TREKKING
IN AFRICA

A GUIDE TO THE FINEST ROU'

SWAN·HILL
PRESS

TREKKING IN AFRICA

A GUIDE TO THE FINEST ROUTES

Texts
Stefano Ardito

Illustrations of the routes
Cristina Franco

Editorial production
Valeria Manferto De Fabianis
Laura Accomazzo

Graphic layout
Clara Zanotti

Translation
Barbara Fisher

Contents

1 Standing on the boundary between Algeria and Libya, the rocky peaks of the Acacus mountains provide the backdrop to a trek on the dunes of the Sahara. Photograph by Anne Conway

2-3 The small group of houses of the village of D'Aït Souka emerges from the vegetation on the Atlas mountain range in Morocco. Photograph by Christophe Boisvieux

First Published in the UK in 1996 by Swan Hill Press, an imprint of Airlife Publishing Ltd.

British Library
Cataloguing in Publication Data
A catalogue record for this book is available from the British Library

ISBN 1 85310 806 5

Printed in Italy by
Milano Stampa, Farigliano (Cn)
in the month of September 1996.

SWAN HILL PRESS
an imprint of Airlife Publishing Ltd.
101 Longden Road,
Shrewsbury SY3 9EB, England

▨	TREK AREA
●	TOWN
•	VILLAGE
▲	MOUNT
⟁	CAMPING SITE
◉	CAMP
⌂	CAVE
Ⓗ	HOTEL
Ⓟ	CAR PARK
] [	PASS
▱	PLATEAU
🏠	REFUGE HUT
☼	ROCK FORMATION
∴	ARCHAEOLOGICAL SITE
Ψ	SPRING
⛈	FOREST STATION
O	NO SETTLEMENTS

INTRODUCTION

6-7 The paths between the Bandiagara plateau and the base of the Dogon Falaise (Mali) skirt bizarre but lovely rock formations. **Photograph by Mario Verin**

Glaciers across the Equator and impenetrable rain forests, elegant rock needles and bizarre-looking plants, the sudden appearance of leopards and buffaloes and the haunting silence of the largest deserts on earth. Asia may offer the visitor its ancient cultures and great mountains, Australia its mineral wonders and coasts, Latin America its rich traditions and the largest forest on earth. No continent, however, offers visitors the emotions stirred by African nature.

A traditional destination for cross-country safaris, expeditions in the Sahara and birdwatching holidays, this continent is also an extraordinary location for lovers of mountains, trekking, hiking.

In the north, overlooking the imperial cities of Morocco, are the harsh rocky peaks of the Atlas mountains, with their Berbers and splendid villages. South east of these the amazing rocky massifs of the Ahaggar, Tibesti and Air interrupt the desert expanses of sand and rock and the precipices and canyons of the Tassili offer an encounter with the oldest and most numerous rock drawings on the entire continent. Where vegetation reappears at the edge of the great desert the falaise, the rocky Bandiagara cliff, cuts the monotonous skyline of the brousse and protects the villages and the extraordinary Dogon culture at its base.

Beyond the desert all changes. In the west overlooking the Atlantic is the solitary pyramid of Mount Cameroon used as a landmark by Phoenicians and Portughese alike. Two thousand kilometers eastwards, within sight of the Indian Ocean and the Red Sea, the barren Semien, Adua and Bale mountains break the Ethiopian plateau. Farther south, the clouds that envelope the sources of the Nile for much of the year conceal the peaks and glaciers of Ruwenzori and the curious forms of Virunga, the volcanoes where the rare mountain gorillas live.

Beyond Lake Victoria rises the volcano of Elgon. The most famous peaks are just a stone's throw away. From the harsh rocky heights of northern Kenya - the Nyiru, Mathews Peak and Poi - to the forests brimming with fauna of the Aberdares and the serrated peaks of Mount Kenya, the most stately summit in Africa and the symbol of the country's national unity. Just over the border, in Tanzania, the square silhouette of Kilimanjaro at 5895 metres marks the highest

point of the continent. Every year thousands upon thousands of visitors, inspired by the words of Ernest Hemingway and Karen Blixen, march towards its lethal screes and ice terraces. Kilimanjaro is flanked by the lovely Meru pyramid, before the horizons become flatter and less harsh. The wooded heights of Malawi precede the magnificent and variegated mountains of South Africa. The awesome walls of the Drakensberg, the harmonious mountains of the Cape, surrounded by ancient farms and vineyards, and the rocky follies of the Cedarbergs lead to the dark expanse of the austral Ocean. On its shores, the Tsitsikamma cliffs and forest offer more high class itineraries to those on foot. However rich in adventure, the history of hiking in Africa is relatively young. For the first of its two centuries'

history it was confused with that of European exploration of the continent. The first episode worthy of mention is the Mungo Park expedition to the banks of the Niger, which reached the river on 20th July 1796. This twenty-five year old Scottish doctor had embarked at Portsmouth one year and two months earlier; after roughly thirty days at sea he reached the coast of Gambia. On 6th October, at the start of the dry season, he left Jonkakonda, the last white trading post to plunge into the lands of the Fula, Mandingo and Bambara. "I heard the cry *Geo affili*, there is the water". Looking forward it was with boundless joy that I saw the object of my mission. The majestic Niger sparkled in the morning sun as wide as the Thames at Westminster. I hurried towards the bank and, after drinking, I spoke fervent prayers of thanks" wrote Mungo Park, recalling the most important moment in his life. In the early nineteenth century the Europeans started to penetrate the heart of Africa by various routes. To the north, on the edge of the Sahara, adventurous travellers defied the bellicose Tuareg and headed for Marrakesh, Djenné, Timbuktu and the other cities reached by the desert caravans. Many thousands of kilometres farther south, the Boer Voortrekkers were starting to leave the Cape for the Karroo plains and the banks of the Orange River. In 1842, two French travellers climbed to the 4620 metres of Ras Dashan, the highest peak in Ethiopia. The most famous expeditions started from Zanzibar and reached the fertile plateaux of Uganda and Kenya and the mysterious sources of the Nile. These travels - Speke and Burton in 1857, Grant and Speke in 1862, Stanley in 1888 - brought the Europeans within sight of the highest mountains. Kilimanjaro, the Olympus of Ethiopia of the Arab geographers, was sighted on 11th May 1848 by the Swiss missionary Johannes Rebmann. Mount Kenya was "discovered" shortly afterwards at the centre of the savannah contended at the time by the Kikuyu and the warfaring Masai.

8 The glaciers of Mount Kibo are the backdrop to the roads trod every day by the Marangu peasants on their way to the fields at the foot of Kilimanjaro. Photograph by Mauro Burzio

8-9 At about 2000 metres on the mountains of equatorial Africa, trekkers advance through fields that man has snatched with difficulty from the forest. This is between Ibanda and the Nyabitaba Hut, on the first leg of the trek to Ruwenzori from Uganda. Photograph by Cl. Jaccoux/ Agence Freestyle

9 top As on the other towering peaks, on Kilimanjaro the scenery at around 4000 metres is dominated by the bizarre forms of the senecious groundsel.
Photograph by Marco Majrani

Farther from the coast and often hidden by mist, Ruwenzori, Ptolemy's mythical "Mountains of the Moon" was sighted by Stanley in 1888. The attempts to climb the mountains started immediately. The German Von Decken, in 1861, made the first unsure attempt at Kilimanjaro; the Hungarian count Teleki in 1886 came within sight of the highest summits of Kilimanjaro and Mount Kenya. The conquest, however, required the best mountaineers. In 1889, the Austrian Ludwig Purtscheller, responsible for considerable feats on the Alps, accompanied the Liepzig topographer Hans Mayer to the 5895 metres of Kibo, the highest point in Africa, promptly rechristened Kaiser Wilhem Spitze.

Ten years later, two guides from Courmayeur led the Scotsman Halford Mackinder up to the 5199 metres of Mount Batian, the highest

competition between the European powers to seize the continent's wealth, the highest peaks witnessed another series of magnificent adventures. The Britains Shipton, Tillman and Wyn Harris tackled the most difficult faces of Mount Kenya and the Frenchmen Coche and Frison-Roche faced the demanding granite needles of the Ahaggar. German expeditions climbed the glaciers of Mount Kibo, the rocky peaks of Mawenzi and the mysterious Spitzkoppe, the "Matterhorn of the south west" with its granite ramparts in the heart of the Namibian desert. In 1943 three Italian prisoners-of-war - Benuzzi, Barsotti and Balletto - wrote an extraordinary page of adventure and poetry with their escape from Nanyuki towards the peaks of Mount Kenya. Between the two wars, an extraordinary observer - Ernest Hemingway - saw and described the

peak in Kenya, along a still today highly respectable route. It was again the experts of Mont Blanc - Laurent and Joseph Petigax, Emile Brocherel, Laurent Ollier - who in 1907 conducted the Duke of the Abruzzi and his companions to the highest peak of the Ruwenzori range, on that occasion dedicated to Margherita, Queen of Italy. The veil of mystery had been lifted but the awe of the great mountains remained.

In the years of the scramble for Africa, the far from dignified

"square peak of Kilimanjaro".
All these names are familiar to those today approaching the peaks and paths of Africa. Just as the writings of Hunt, Hillary, Diemberger and Messner accompany the modern high altitude pilgrims in the Himalayas and Karakoram, *The Snows of Kilimanjaro* by Hemingway, *Fuga sul Kenya* by Benuzzi, *That Untravelled World* by Shipton and the *Carnets Sahariens* by Frison-Roche are often - quite rightly - tucked away in the rucksack of those hiking in Africa. The history of the white man's

adventures is not the only nor the main reason for interest in these mountains. Amidst the great mountains of Asia man's memories and monuments are what most amaze: the mosques of Shigar and Chitral, the Hindu temples of Kathmandu, the Buddhist monasteries of Tibet, Bhutan and Ladakh. Africa has the beaten earth constructions of the Atlas, the Tassili drawings, the Coptic churches of the Ethiopian mountains. It is nature that generates the most excitement. The extraordinary Ruwenzori and

Virunga rain forest and the bizarre-looking lobelia and senecious, the red rocks of the Nelion and the ice stairs of Mount Kibo, will never be forgotten by this writer and will remain in the heart of every visitor to these mountains. The sudden appearance of buffaloes and leopards, steinbok and antilopes, gelada baboons and vultures forges a bond between the mountains of Africa and every trekker who has walked their slopes. Hopefully these natural treasures will survive for our children and grandchildren.

10 The fiery scenery of the Sahara reappears thousands of kilometres farther south in Namibia as can be seen in this lovely view of Fish River Canyon, the second largest on earth after that created by the Colorado River in Arizona.
Photograph by Mauro Burzio

10-11 At the two ends of the continent the landscape becomes barren and austere. In this picture a caravan of trekkers is on a meharée *at the foot of the Hoggar range (Algeria).*
Photograph by Didier Givois

WHO CAN TREK?

Hiking in the great mountains, along the coasts and in the spectacular African deserts is not just sport.

A trek in the Himalayas or Karakoram is always a great adventure among fascinating peoples and cultures, but a trek in Africa offers the possibility, above all, to gain first-hand knowledge of the remarkable nature of this continent. Far from the world of the savannah you will find scenery, fauna and flora of exceptional interest. From the Atlas to the Semien and from Tassili to the Cape mountains, trekking is also an opportunity to get to know ethnic groups, customs and local traditions.

It is important to remember that trekking is, nonetheless, a sport and as such requires a certain amount of physical preparation. Newcomers should remember that mountain hiking also makes psychological demands.

The beautiful sunrises and sunsets, the memories of evenings passed around the camp fire and splendid views from hills and mountain tops dim the memory (ours and that of others) of different moments. The fatigue brought on by the weight of the rucksack, the sun beating down inexorably and descents, maybe in the pouring rain, that never seem to end. On the Alps, you may miss the marked path or sleep on the floor of overcrowded refuge huts, but in Africa the hardships can be far greater for the size of these mountains and the traveller's sense of bewilderment. Paths can be made more difficult by mud or snow; the weather on the "African Giants" can change with incredible speed. Someone wrote that mountains and trekking are schools of life. We would say that being ready to put up with delays, the unforeseen and inconvenience is a must for those approaching these paths.

HOW TO PREPARE

Those who regularly go hiking, mountaineering or practise other endurance sports such as jogging or cross-country skiing will have no difficulty in meeting the physical demands of trekking.

For the not so young, accustomed to a predominantly sedentary lifestyle, a training programme is recommended, preceded perhaps by a medical check up.

Before an African hike, train on the hills or mountains close to home. Especially if you are heading for the highest peaks (Kilimanjaro, Kenya, Ruwenzori, Semien) it is advisable to get acclimatized to the high altitudes and, if possible, spend a few nights in mountain huts above 3000 metres. Even those who run or hike regularly on the plain should do some training that includes considerable vertical ascents and descents: the muscles and breath work differently on the plain! In the Alps many hikes include snow fields, rocks or nailed sections but only a few African treks offer technical demands on snow-fields, glaciers or rocky trails.

The routes up to the peaks of Ruwenzori and Mount Kenya are, however, true mountaineering ascents on rock and ice, reserved for those with sufficient experience or accompanied by a guide. Mountaineering experience can never be improvised. One can learn by attending a course organized by a mountaineering association or alpine guides, or by choosing an organized and properly accompanied trek.

12 top A group of trekkers, together with some porters, crosses the desert Saddle plateau, approaching the Kilimanjaro peak. Photograph by Didier Givois

12 bottom A group of trekkers tackles an undemanding climb through the rock formations of the Gebel Sarrho range in Morocco. Photograph by Marco Majrani

WHICH TREK TO CHOOSE

The altitude, the type of natural and human habitat, geographic location and the degree of technical and physical demands are the bases for a choice of trek on all the mountains in the world. Although marked on the Alps, contrasts become extreme in Africa. The desert environment of the mountainous chains of the Sahara is very different from that of the damp high altitude forests of Ruwenzori, the Aberdares, and Mount Kenya. The austere welcome of the Tuareg and Berbers in the Atlas mountains has little in common with the smiles of the mountain-dwellers of Ethiopia and eastern Africa.

The length and physical demands of a trek vary. Everyone must make a personal choice. As much information as possible has been included in the presentation of the treks in this book to make the choice easier.

THE TRIP

Leaving for the Sahara or black Africa means that in just a few hours' flight you will approach one of the most interesting natural and human environments on earth.

The difference in climate, in smells, in sensations make it an exciting and always new adventure, even for the most expert traveller. This book does not provide information on the prices and routes for your flight to Africa. Those new to trekking in this part of the world should remember two crucial factors when planning their journey.

The first and most important is the time of year. In the Africa of the Sahara and pre-Sahara you hike during the European winter or, at the very most, in the middle seasons. An exception to this are the highest peaks of the Atlas, very popular also in July and August. Even for a climb to Mount Toubkal, however, the months preceding the summer offer the trekker more congenial conditions. On the mountains of Ethiopia there is just one dry season from mid October to the end of May. From the beginning of March, however, matters are complicated by sporadic but violent showers arriving from the Indian Ocean.

In eastern Africa (Kenya, Uganda, eastern Zaire, Tanzania) the violent rainfalls during the wet season discourage walking between mid March and early June (great rains) and between October and December (small rains). The high season for safaris in the parks coincides with that for trekking on Kilimanjaro, Mount Kenya and the nearby mountains. The same applies for the Ruwenzori and Virunga massifs that separate the savannah and hills of eastern Africa from the Congo river basin. On these mountains rain and mud (and snowfalls at high altitudes) are faithful companions of mountaineers and trekkers all the year round. At the extreme south of the continent the seasons are simply the reverse of those in the United States and Europe although the right time to start varies from trek to trek. Those at low altitudes, such as Fish River Canyon, must be done during the local winter, i.e. the European summer. On the Otter Trail and the treks on the Cape and Transkei coasts, the nearby ocean makes the climate acceptable all year round. In the mountains, on the other hand, you can choose. For South African trekkers the high season for the Drakensberg paths corresponds to the local summer and, therefore, the European winter. Nonetheless, many foreign hikers find the humid heat of January and February on these mountains too much and prefer the

13 top Mist is common on the mountains of equatorial Africa and turns the lobelia and groundsel into fascinating spectral forms. Here, on Mount Kenya, at about 4000 metres, the path climbs up Mackinder Valley. Photograph by Stefano Ardito

13 centre The sun and a blue sky accompany a group of trekkers on their way to Wolfsberg's Arch, in the fascinating barren South African Cedarberg mountains. Photograph by Hein von Horsten/ABPL

13 bottom Between 3000 and 4000 metres the paths of Mount Kenya pass through spectacular barren mountain steppes. The photo shows a trekker and his Kikuyu guide on the path to the Liki Hut, on the Sirimon route. Photograph by Stefano Ardito

winter or middle seasons. I would agree with them. It should not be forgotten that the frequent summer · thunderstorms on the "dragons' mountains" intensify the spectacle of torrents, waterfalls and flowers in bloom. Compared with the great mountains of Asia, hiking in Africa poses far fewer bureaucratic problems. Numerous countries require an entry visa, but permits for hiking and climbing are quickly obtained directly at the gates of the various national parks. On some mountains, Kilimanjaro in particular, the cost of permits has become very high. It is perfectly legitimate that a country such as Tanzania should expect "rich" Americans and Europeans heading for the "Roof of Africa" to pay, but 350 dollars for just five days in the mountains really seems an exaggeration. At the extreme south of the continent, in South Africa and Namibia, early booking is a must. The limited number of visitors allowed on the paths - the Otter Trail and Fish River Canyon are often fully "booked" a year in advance - makes access difficult for foreigners who do not contact a specialist agency in time. The reservation of a number of places to be allocated at the last moment would certainly make matters easier for those coming from afar.

ALONE OR IN A GROUP?

Geographically distant, extremely different in environment and characteristics from the mountains at home, the great African massifs pose very different organizational and psychological problems from those of the Alps. Various solutions are possible according to personal experience. There are undeniable advantages in going with an organized group. New travelling companions, somebody else who looks after the flight reservations, visas and on-the-spot organization; in the company of an expert (a mountain guide in particular) even the least expert hikers can tackle rocks and glaciers safely. Baggage is entrusted to porters or beasts of burden; the trekker carries only a

"daypack" with anorak, a change of clothes, camera and a little food. The negative aspects are the higher price and the fact that very probably contacts with the locals will be few. The best solution for many is to arrive in Africa without using an agency and to engage a guide, porters and/or beasts of burden locally. Certainly more economical, this system is recommended only in certain areas with a longstanding tradition and expertise (the best examples are Kenya and Morocco) and elsewhere is reserved only for

those with a certain trekking experience.
At the other extreme comes fully self-sufficient trekking: travelling with food and kitchen equipment.
This is, of course, only suited to hikers trained to the fatigues of Anglo Saxon-style backpacking and means that accessories must be limited to the very minimum.
It is worth remembering, however, that this can be done only in certain areas, Mount Kenya, Ethiopia, the Atlas and the paths of Namibia and South Africa to start with.
In many areas - Ruwenzori, Tassili, Virunga, Aberdares - the presence of a guide (usually an armed ranger) is compulsory for all. On Kilimanjaro both guide and porters are obligatory. Climate, distances and the impossibility to procure food make backpacking on mountains such as Ruwenzori extremely laborious and actually impracticable. It should also be remembered that in Africa there are no inviting refuge huts such as those of the Alps, nor is there the dense network of small hotels and tea shops found along the most popular routes in Nepal.

PORTERS

On the mountains of Africa the engaging and use of porters is usually less complicated by rules and conventions than in the Himalayas or Karakoram.
There are, however, certain principles, dictated more by common sense than by tradition, that should be respected.
The load, contained in a bag or plastic drum, must not (save for special agreements) weigh more than 15 or 20 kilos: every porter must add his own belongings to yours, plus food for himself and his colleagues. The guide or ranger's baggage is usually also entrusted to the porters.
Where the fees are not fixed by law, the bargaining must take into account any days of road transfer, the price of public transport and board. At the end of the trek a tip and/or gifts of clothes or equipment are always welcome.

14 top A hiker stops in the upper Mackinder Valley near the impressive rocky Terere and Sendeyo peaks. Photograph by Stefano Ardito

14 bottom Above the edge of the rain forest on Kilimanjaro the landscape becomes august and desert-like. A group of porters is heading for the Horombo Hut and the Kibo peak. Photograph by Marco Majrani

15 top The paths on Ruwenzori are notoriously awkward because of the vegetation, the slippery terrain and the mud. In the photo a Zairese ranger accompanies a party of trekkers towards Lac Gris (4300 metres). Photograph by Marco Majrani

15 centre On many African ranges the absence of or poorly kept refuge huts makes the use of a tent obligatory. The photo shows a camp on the Zairese side of Ruwenzori at about 4000 metres above sea level. Photograph by Marco Majrani

15 bottom Up to 3000 metres treks to Kilimanjaro pass through the rain forest. The photo shows a party on the Machame route, at about 2700 metres above sea level. Photograph by Stefano Ardito

CLOTHING AND EQUIPMENT

Lightness and comfort are of course the priorities for the a trekker's clothing. Baggage must be prepared with due consideration for the altitude of the chosen trek and the time of year. In many cases, especially on the longer routes, treks on the great mountains of Africa offer the hiker very marked contrasts in climate and exposure to sunlight. In just a few days you may pass from the 40°C+ of the savannah around Kilimanjaro and Mount Kenya to the cold humid climate at 4000 and 5000 metres. At high altitudes, here as everywhere, there are great differences between day and night. On the mountains of the Sahara, despite the lower altitude, these contrasts are even more noticeable. Those with no desert experience should remember that in the Sahara in winter the climate is usually much colder than the inexperienced traveller is likely to imagine. At the average altitudes of the African mountains (i.e. between 2000 and 4000 metres) the best solution is a pair of cloth trousers (if possible looser and more comfortable than jeans) with a change into shorts for the hottest hours of the day and pile trousers for the coldest times. The traditional plus-fours are comfortable and can be worn with tights in severe cold. A woollen or pile jumper can be worn over the classical wool shirt or a more modern synthetic sweater. At all altitudes a waterproof suit (jacket and trousers) in Goretex or similar material is essential. Completing the list are a wool hat and a cloth one for the sun, a pair of gloves in wool or pile and a pair of sunglasses. Essential accessories include a water bottle, spare boot laces and a multipurpose knife (Swiss army type). It is also important to have a torch, better if it is a helmet lamp. The sleeping bag must be chosen with consideration for the coldest days of the trip. The rucksack is another important piece of equipment. Trekkers carrying most of their baggage with them will need a capacious one (70 litres upwards). The daypack of those travelling on an organized trek can be much smaller. As on the Alps, footwear is crucial: the wrong choice may ruin an otherwise memorable trek. It is important that the footwear be tested in the previous months. Today leather or synthetic climbing boots are used by all and are the best solution for nearly all our treks. For high altitudes, and to avoid problems in the event of unexpected snowfalls, it may be wise to take a pair of plastic mountaineering boots. The ascent to the peaks of Ruwenzori and Mount Kenya requires the necessary mountaineering gear (rope, harnesses, karabiners, cords, helmet, crampons and ice-axe). Ski poles are always useful, even better if adjustable.

FINDING ONE'S WAY

Those used to hiking on the Alps are accustomed to seeing painted indications and signs or the traditional, welcome rock pyramids. On the snowy stretches of the classic routes, the traces of the mountaineers and hikers gone before are usually clearly visible. Maps are usually recent and show all signposting. More information can be obtained from refuge huts and tourist offices.

In Africa the situation is very different. Painted indications are unheard of, rock pyramids rare, maps - save for few exceptions - are approximative and inaccurate. Only occasionally, unlike the Himalayas, do the paths used by trekkers correspond with the long established routes still used by the local inhabitants and caravans. Orientation is usually easy on the most popular massifs, where the paths are nearly always clear.

In the impenetrable forests of Ruwenzori and Virunga, or in the rocky maze of the Tefedest or Tassili, the company of a guide - usually compulsory - is the best insurance against trouble.

The lack of good maps makes a compass and altimeter slightly less helpful than on the Alps.

MEDICAL PROBLEMS

Hiking in Africa poses a series of problems similar to those of trekking on the Alps or in the North American or Japanese mountains. Blisters and cramp, frostbite and sprains are problems common whether you are trekking on the paths of Kilimanjaro or hiking on the Dolomites or at the foot of Everest.

On the highest mountains, the fast climb from sea level to 4000 or 5000 metres is a further problem that should be approached with proper training before departure, a schedule including a few days for acclimatization and a constant attention to any signs of mountain sickness or edema.

As in the Himalayas or Karakoram an immediate descent is a princely remedy in the event of indispositions of this nature.

The Sahara is one of the healthiest environments on earth and much of Namibia and South Africa (with

the exception of the savannahs of Etosha, Natal and Kruger) poses no particular problems. In the rest of Africa, however, the traveller, and hence the mountaineer and trekker too, will face varied and very serious health hazards.

In most of the continent, besides vaccinations against yellow fever, typhus and cholera, an anti-malaria prophylaxis is absolutely essential; the medicines most suited to the malaria stocks present in the area should be used: some populations of anopheles resistant to chloroquine exist in vast areas of Kenya, Tanzania, Zaire and Uganda.

No medicine abolishes the need for the standard precautions to be taken by those travelling in much of Africa and Asia. To drink water that has not been disinfected or boiled or eat unwashed fruit or vegetables is looking for trouble. Swimming in stagnant water will

expose you to the risk of contacting with schistosoma, a potentially lethal parasite.

IN CASE OF TROUBLE

On the Alps and the other mountain chains of Europe, a remarkable percentage of accidents is due to the carelessness of hikers on terrain erroneously considered "easy".

On the mountains of Africa exposed paths, slippery, muddy stretches and steep screes with precariously poised rocks require the utmost caution. The attention should be even greater than in the Alps as the evacuation of the sick and injured down the valley and to hospital is always a serious problem in Africa.

PHOTOGRAPHIC EQUIPMENT

Sunsets and animals, panoramas and villages, the faces of a thousand different ethnic groups. There are thousands of possible photographs in Africa and on its mountains and potentially the amount of equipment needed is huge. For the hiker-photographer baggage weight is the main restriction to be considered. This limit applies to all even though it is far more severe for the do-it-yourself trekker than for those using porters or beasts of burden.
The essential choice for the hiker -

in the middle of the day.
Among the reversible films, the best are low sensitivity ones i.e. between 25 and 100 ASA.
Those hiking with porters and beasts of burden can leave some of their equipment in their baggage. Extreme care must always be taken to protect photographic material from blows and sunlight.

one that means a difference of one or two kilos in the rucksack -
is between a compact 35 mm camera, capable despite its light weight of capturing panoramas and the most important moments of the trek, and a reflex 35 mm with two or three lens, serving for a reportage true and proper. In the latter case the lens must be chosen carefully: a 28 mm wide angle, a 35 mm or 50 mm and a 105 or 135 telephoto lens (or a 70-150 mm or similar zoom) will be of most use.
The abundant African fauna also makes a 200 mm or 300 mm telephoto lens advisable.
A lens for macrophotography may be useful for the flora.
Filters (skylight or UV and polarizer) are fundamental, as well as a small tripod, important when fixing the magic colours of sunset or dawn on film and photographing inside the tropical forest, always fascinating but invariably dark even

RESPECT THE LANDSCAPE, RESPECT THE LOCAL PEOPLE

"Even the excessive noise you make in the camp in the evening, the glaring bright colours of your clothes can reduce the experience of the wilderness for others treading these paths." This, together with considerations of a more technical nature, is the advice given to hikers by the official guide to the paths of the Grand Canyon: one of the vastest and most impressive wildernesses in the world. "Nothing makes natural scenery seem inhabited like a group of clearly visible tents... the advantages of blending in with the landscape always

prevail." Thus addresses his readers John Hart the author of *Walking Softly in the Wilderness*, the hiking manual of the American Sierra Club. In Africa this advice is even more important. The summits of Mount Kenya and Kilimanjaro, the forests of Cameroon and Virunga, the rocks of the Drakensbergs and the Ahaggar are among the most spectacular natural monuments on earth and remain - over and above the presence of the trekker and the mountaineer - solitary and wild places that must be respected at all times. The careful hiker will thus refrain from any damaging behaviour and also vigilate over the guides and porters, frequently less aware of the need to eliminate waste properly or carry it back down to the valley and using gas or petrol stoves instead of the traditional wood fires. The plateaux at the foot of the great mountains, on the other hand, are not a wilderness devoid of human presence. The fertile

hills of Cameroon and Mount Kenya, eastern Zaire and Uganda suffer from serious overpopulation. This problem is common to far less wealthy areas such as the savannahs of Tanzania, the hills of the Zulus, the high lands of Ethiopia. More so than tourism or the "commercial" poaching that has caused a dramatic fall in the numbers of elephants and the near extinction of the rhinoceros, it is the increasing pressure of the population that is endangering the nature of the last remaining wildernesses in Africa and hence also the forests on the slopes of the major peaks. This phenomenon is also to be seen in much of the Third World and causes everywhere -

from the Himalayas to the Amazon - deforestation, pollution, the extinction of rare and precious animal species and land erosion. Before problems of such dimensions, the responsibility of and possibilities for hikers or mountaineers to act are extremely limited. The tragic recent experience of Rwanda, Somalia and other countries shows unfortunately how much the policies of most western governments with regard to Africa still leave much to be desired.
As in other parts of the world, and in particular the Himalayas and Karakoram, correct handling of the protected areas can play a positive role, combining for the local population the financial benefits brought by tourism with the sacrifices in pasture lands, hunting and forest exploitation. On Kilimanjaro, on Mount Kenya, on Ruwenzori, in the Semien, the hiker arriving from afar can feel part of a positive and

important mechanism. Respect cannot and must not only be for the woods, animals and scenery. At least equal in importance is the respect of the traditions and culture, religious beliefs and taboos of the African peoples. Everywhere you should learn and respect the local rites, holy places and religious beliefs, maintaining an attitude very different from that of the aggressive tourist hunting for pictures at any price. Guides and porters must be treated with the due respect, without forgetting that in Africa and Europe alike being employed by someone is very different from slavery. Lastly you should refrain from purchasing antique objects of art and the hides or other parts of animals in danger of extinction. Apart from the confiscation of the object, anyone found in the possession of ivory, leopard skins or sea-turtle shells quite rightly risks large fines both on departure and arrival.

19 left An intense portrait of a young girl of the Kenyan Turkana tribe.
Photograph by Marcello Bertinetti/ White Star Archive

19 top right The remarkable assortment of ethnic groups is another great attraction of treks in Africa. The picture shows an encounter *with some Tuareg and their camels loaded with salt in the Mali desert.*
Photograph by Werner Gartung/ Wings/Overseas

19 bottom right Two women at Ti-n-Iddr baking bread in a traditional wood oven.
Photograph by Stefano Ardito

ALONG THE PATHS OF TENERIFE

Lava, forests and scenery on
the green island of the Canaries.

"The day was starting to appear as we left the Cuevo del Hielo. We then observed a phenomenon fairly common on high mountains, made even more notable by the position of the volcano. A blanket of white clouds concealed the Ocean and the lowlands of the island from our view. The huge pyramid of the Pico, the volcanic peaks of Lanzarote, Fuerteventura and the island of La Palma rose like isolated rocks from this sea of steam." Thus, at dawn on 22 June 1799, the German naturalist Alexander Humboldt started on the final stretch of his climb to the Pico de Teide peak, the highest point on the Canary Islands and the whole Spanish territory. After camping out "in the freezing cold even though we had the lovely African sky above us" the party made a detour from the straightest route to the top to visit this remarkable cave lined with ice. The ascent then proceeded along the "broken lava of malpaìs", with an "extremely tiring, steep route along which blocks of lava constantly fall away beneath our feet", where "even the local guides, desperately slow, would sit down to rest every ten minutes". At last Humboldt and his companions sat on the broken rocks of the peak, 3,718 metres above sea level. Before them, within reach, was the lovely small Teide crater, with its crystals and fumaroles. Exhausting but presenting no mountaineering difficulties, the climb to the volcano that dominates Tenerife was for the German naturalist and his French friend Aimé Bonpland, a welcome break on their long voyage to the Americas, where the two were to make one of the most famous naturalistic expeditions in history, exploring the Orinoco basin and attempting to climb Mount Chimborazo, the volcano 6,300 metres high thought at the time to be the highest peak on earth.

During the ascent and the descent afterwards Humboldt was to have repeated opportunities to admire the varied nature of the island. His definition of the Orotava Valley as "the loveliest place on earth" is quoted at every step to today's visitors to Tenerife and may seem an exaggeration at the first encounter with the mass of hotels in the large tourist resorts on the island. But this impression will change as the varied scenery, the monuments in the historical towns and a pleasant climate all year round make the island a paradise for the traveller even today. It may seem odd to start a book on treks in Africa with two itineraries on Spanish soil but although the archipelago of the Canaries is Spanish in population, tradition and culture it belongs geographically to Africa. Fuerteventura and Lanzarote, the most "African" islands in terms of climate and scenery, are just a hundred kilometres from the coast of Morocco. Visited by the Phoenicians, the "Fortunate Islands" described by Ptolemy were rediscovered later by Arabs and Genoese. The conquest began in 1402 with the landing of the Frenchman Béthencourt and cost the Europeans 50 years of bloody battle. At the end of this time, the complex and mysterious native civilization, the Guanches, had been totally wiped out. During the long centuries of the Spanish Empire the Canaries (in particular Las Palmas de Gran Canaria and Santa Cruz de Tenerife) provided important safe landing places for cargo and war ships heading for the Americas, which stopped here to stock up on food and wine. A very similar role was played farther north by the Azores for the Portuguese navigators sailing to India and Brazil. The scenery of Tenerife is still

20-21 The warm light of sunset colours the unusual Piedras Amarillas towers. This is at 2,120 metres above sea level in the heart of the Cañadas del Teide National Park. Photograph by Stefano Ardito

22-23 Looking onto the blue Atlantic Ocean, the white houses of Taganana greet the trekker at the end of the route that starts from Playa del Hidalgo and passes Carboneras, Taborno and Afur.

23 top
The extraordinary view from the path across the Cañadas del Teide from Portillo to Piedras Amarillas alternates sandy open spaces and spectacular towers of lava.

23 bottom The third highest peak on Tenerife, the Montaña de Guajara (2,717 metres), is reached on easy scenic paths from Cañadas del Teide or from the Vilaflor side.
Photographs by Stefano Ardito

pleasing to the eye although the island has long become one of the most popular "charter paradises" for Europeans in search of a sunny break during the cold winter months. Just a short climb from the large hotels of Puerto de la Cruz and Playa de Las Americas are the attractive towns of Orotava and La Laguna with their colonial architecture, the vineyards and banana plantations on the north of the island and the *laurisilva* forests on the Anaga peninsula, so reminiscent of the appearance and fragrances of the Mediterranean maquis.

Higher up, above two thousand metres, the traveller is greeted by a wild and totally different spectacle. That of the Cañadas del Teide and the majestic volcano cone that rises to 3,718 metres above sea level.

The crater has been protected since 1954 in one of the major national parks in Spain (spread over 13,451 hectares) and is crossed by a scenic asphalted road. Lovely paths lead visitors into an unusual and at times plainly lunar landscape which at dawn and dusk turns all shades of yellow, ochre and red.

The best way to end a visit to the Cañadas is to climb to the top of Mount Teide; this is done every year by thousands of tourists who use the cableway that rises to 3,550 metres but should really be done on foot, in particular in the magic hours of dawn and dusk, to enjoy a spectacle identical to that admired by Humboldt and Bonpland.

In winter when the mountain is snowclad and the cableway is closed, the climb to the top of Teide requires mountaineering equipment and experience as well as clothing suited to the altitude and wind, often extremely violent as on all the great solitary mountains.

However, Tenerife has more to offer excursion-lovers than its highest peak and the extraordinary

crater that surrounds it. Enjoyable treks of different lengths can be made nearly all over the island. One of the areas that deserves special attention is that of the fragrant forests of Canary pine between Vilaflor and the Cañadas, the wild Teno peninsula forming the westernmost limit of the island, the spectacular Anaga peninsula

a stone's throw from La Laguna and Santa Cruz.

This peninsula, dear to both the *tirfenos* hikers and to those arriving from Europe,has many treks and surprises in store for those who set off along its paths.

A bus can be taken along the road that climbs to the Cruz de Carmen and the Pico del Inglès; an easy descent is then made on the magnificent paths down to the most picturesque villages on the island and the specatacular, rocky coast of Taganana and Bajamar.

USEFUL INFORMATION

Duration: the trek on Pico de Teide takes three or four days. The Anaga peninsula offers numerous one-day treks.

Altitude: from sea level to 3,718 metres.

Period: all year round. From November to April the climb on Pico de Teide is a mountaineering one. In the same period the Altavista refuge hut is closed.

Formalities: none.

Difficulty: apart from the Teide in winter there are no technical problems. Parts of the Anaga paths are exposed.

Physical demands: the climb to Pico de Teide is tiring because of the altitude. The other legs are average-low in difficulty.

Equipment: normal trekking gear.

Access routes: the efficient TITSA bus network connects all the towns on the island (including Orotava, Cañadas del Teide, Pico del Inglès and Taganana) with Santa Cruz de Tenerife and the tourist resorts on the island. As there is no hotel at Portillo, at the end of the first leg trekkers must descend by bus to Orotava and return the next day.

Guides and porters: some of the hotels in Tenerife offer organized excursions on the islands paths.

Variations and other peaks: the three highest peaks on the island, Pico de Teide (3,718 metres), Pico Viejo (3,140 metres) and Montaña de Guajara (2,717 metres) are on the first trek described. The numerous possible variations to this route include the interesting descent to Vilaflor from Degollada de Guajara. In winter the Altavista refuge hut is closed, making the leg devoted to the Teide longer and more exhausting. The Anaga peninsula offers a wide range of paths. One of these climbs on fragile terrain and with moutaineering passages to the Roque de Taborno.

In the event of trouble: there is no mountain rescue and you must contact the rangers of the Cañadas del Teide National Park or the Guardia Civil (tel. 062) and the Policia National (tel. 091).

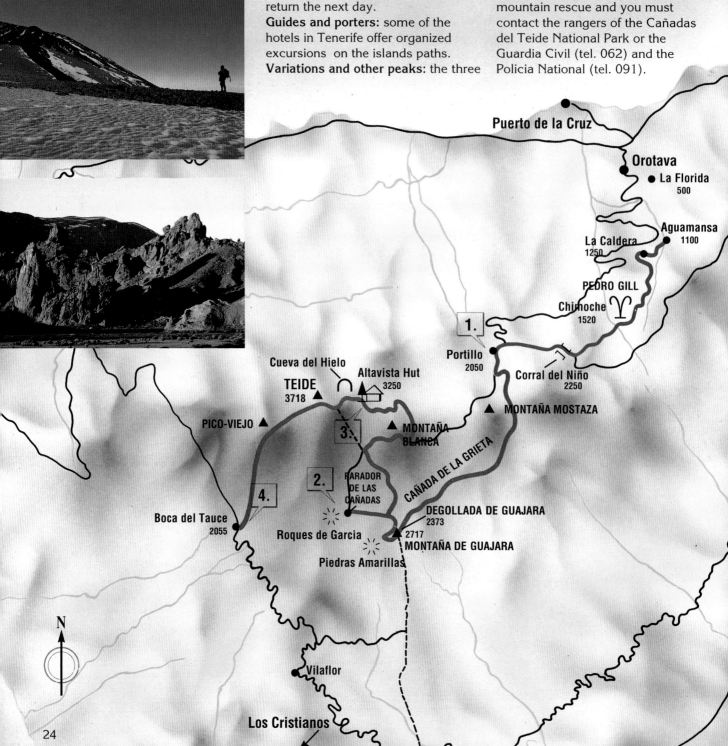

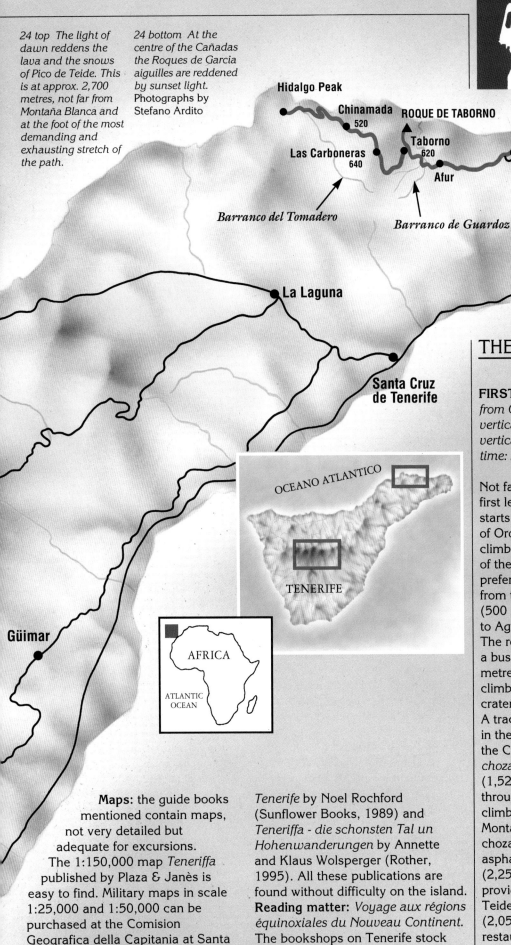

24 top The light of dawn reddens the lava and the snows of Pico de Teide. This is at approx. 2,700 metres, not far from Montaña Blanca and at the foot of the most demanding and exhausting stretch of the path.

24 bottom At the centre of the Cañadas the Roques de Garcia aiguilles are reddened by sunset light. Photographs by Stefano Ardito

Hidalgo Peak

Chinamada
520

ROQUE DE TABORNO

Playa de Benijo

Almaciga

Taborno
620

Las Carboneras
640

Taganana
150

Barranco del Tomadero

Afur

Barranco de Guardoz

La Laguna

Santa Cruz de Tenerife

OCEANO ATLANTICO

TENERIFE

AFRICA

ATLANTIC OCEAN

Güimar

THE TEIDE PATH

FIRST DAY
from Orotava to Portillo
vertical ascent: 1,150 metres
vertical descent: 200 metres
time: 5 hours

Not far from Puerto de la Cruz, the first leg of the climb to the Teide starts with a visit to the historic town of Orotava before a long and pleasant climb through the woods to the edge of the volcanic plateau. Those preferring a longer itinerary can start from the foot of La Florida (500 metres) or even from Orotava to Aguamansa along a quiet road. The route recommended starts with a bus ride to Aguamansa (1,100 metres) and from here a half hour climb takes you to the secondary crater La Caldera (1,250 metres). A track through the woods advances in the Barranco de Pedro Gil, passing the Chimoche spring and reaching the *choza* (picnic area) of Chimoche (1,520 metres). From here you zigzag through the coniferous woods, climbing at length towards the Montaña de Limon and another choza. A forest road leads to the asphalted road near Corral del Niño (2,250 metres). An hour on this road, providing a magnificent view of the Teide, leads to the Portillo pass (2,050 metres) and a number of restaurants plus the Park Visitor Centre. As there is no hotel, unless you have a tent, you must take the bus to Orotava or Parador de Las Canarias.

Maps: the guide books mentioned contain maps, not very detailed but adequate for excursions.
The 1:150,000 map *Teneriffa* published by Plaza & Janès is easy to find. Military maps in scale 1:25,000 and 1:50,000 can be purchased at the Comision Geografica della Capitania at Santa Cruz de Tenerife.
Guide books: *Excursiones a piè por Tenerife* by Manuel Mora Morales (Globo 1994), *Landscapes of Tenerife* by Noel Rochford (Sunflower Books, 1989) and *Teneriffa - die schonsten Tal un Hohenwanderungen* by Annette and Klaus Wolsperger (Rother, 1995). All these publications are found without difficulty on the island.
Reading matter: *Voyage aux régions équinoxiales du Nouveau Continent*. The bookshops on Tenerife stock *Viaje a las Islas Canarias* (F. Lemus, 1995) an excerpt in Spanish of the chapter on the visit to the island and the ascent of Pico de Teide.

SECOND DAY
from Portillo
to the Montaña de Guajara
and to Parador de las Cañadas
vertical ascent: 780 metres
vertical descent: 720 metres
time: 6 hours

Leaving the green slopes down to Orotava and Puerto de la Cruz behind you, on the second day of the trek you will become accustomed to the remarkable scenery of the Cañadas, the wide volcanic caldera that surrounds the Pico. This otherwise very short leg is completed with the scenic climb of the Montaña de Guajara, at 2,717 metres is the third highest peak on the island. From the Park Visitor Centre follow a dirt track, closed to cars by a barrier, that plunges amid the lava. Go right at a fork and proceed, with a lovely view of the lava of the Montaña Mostaza. Once past the rocks of the Montaña Colorada and the Cueva de Diego Hernandez you will see the Canada de la Grieta and its abandoned pens. A section in descent leads to the fork (2,180 metres) where the path to the Degollada de Guajara pass (2,373 metres) branches off to the left. Proceed towards the right, leaving a path to Vilaflor to the left and you will come to the scenic Montaña de Guajara (2,717 metres) which deserves a halt. Another path descends westwards to Degollada de Ucanca and then plunges steeply northwards in the direction of the characteristic Piedras Amarillas. You come out onto an asphalt road; go right to the towers, then follow a path to Parador de las Cañadas (2,184 metres). A short walk from the hotel are the Roques de Garcia, a group of characteristic rocky towers particularly enchanting at sunset.

26 top The Altavista Hut, a solid brick construction at 3,250 metres welcomes the trekkers at the end of the steep climb to the top of Pico de Teide. Photograph by Stefano Ardito

26 bottom A trekker follows the easy path along the Pico de Teide crater, a few steps from the summit. Photograph by Stefano Ardito

THIRD DAY
from Parador de las Cañadas
to the Altavista refuge hut
vertical ascent: 1,150 metres
vertical descent: 70 metres
time: 6 hours

A variable day, tiring on the final stretch, leads to the Altavista refuge hut, a convenient backup point at the foot of the Teide peak. Trekkers spend the night at the hut so as to arrive on the top before the hordes of tourists on the cableway. From Parador return to Piedras Amarillas and proceed for about 1 kilometre on the trail at the foot of Montaña de Guajara. Go left at a fork and proceed towards Pico de Teide until you come again to the asphalted road not far from the base of the cableway. Follow this for just over 2 kilometres to the right, on a scenic route made joyless by the traffic to a small rocky pass. Just on the other side a large white sign indicates the start (2,350 metres) of the trail that climbs to Montaña Blanca. Follow this for a quarter of an hour and then turn left on one or other of the two steep paths that avoid the long bends of the road returned to at about 2,700 metres. A sign indicates the start of the path that rises in large hairpin bends to the Altavista refuge hut (3,250 metres). The best end to the day is a walk (3/4 hour return) to the Cueva del Hielo, a cave lined with ice.

FOURTH DAY
from the Altavista refuge hut
to the Pico del Teide
and Boca de Tauce
vertical ascent: 460 metres
vertical descent:.1,650 metres
time: 6 hours

Another long and spectacular leg offering an encounter with the two volcano craters, the remarkable views from the peak and the solitary descent to Boca del Tauce and the road. Set off in the first light of morning along the wide path through spikes of lava that leads to the foot of the summit and then proceed towards the peak (3,718 metres). Descend to the highest station on the cableway (3,555 metres) and continue westwards on the wide Rambleta path. Once at the scenic point at the end of the path, descend steeply to the saddle between the two Teide peaks, from where you climb again briefly to the southern peak of Pico Viejo (3,107 metres) and a large pyramid of rocks. After admiring the Pico Viejo crater descend along a good path to the twin Narices (Nose) del Teide (2,598 metres) craters. A fast descent on the lava will bring you to the clearing at the foot of the volcano. The path crosses the Chafari valley then becomes a wide trail to Boca del Tauce (2,055 metres). Proceed by bus or hitch hike to Vilaflor or Santiago del Teide.

FROM PUNTA DEL HIDALGO TO TABORNO AND TAGANANA

Descend in a deep valley with a number of isolated houses to the cool waters of the Barranco de Guardoz and climb again to Afur (320 metres), another charming little village. Set off along the road again, turning onto a dirt road and then go down through the fields to the village of Taganana (150 metres).
The walk should be continued to the houses of Almiciga and the lovely stony beach of Beniyo (half an hour extra).

ONE-DAY TREK
*From the Punta del Hidalgo
to Taborno and to Taganana
vertical ascent and descent: 850 metres
time: 6 and a half - 7 hours*

This is one of the longest and most pleasant treks on the Anaga peninsula and goes from the vineyards of Tacoronte and Bajamar to the foot of the spectacular Roque de Taborno continuing to Taganana passing some of the remotest villages on Tenerife. The starting point is the Playa del Hidalgo, along a descending trail dominated by the towers of Los Hermanos.
After crossing a bridge over the Barranco de Tomadero, climb on a steep and aerial path dug in the rock. At the end of the most tiring stretch are the few houses of Chinamada (520 metres) from where you proceed on a dirt track towards Las Carboneras (640 metres).
You can avoid the road by taking a path to Taborno (620 metres) from where in just a few minutes you come to a viewpoint overlooking Roque de Taborno.

27 left Nicknamed "the Matterhorn of Tenerife" by trekkers, the Roque de Taborno tower overlooks the northern coast of the island.

27 top right The white houses of Tagarna contrast with the green mountains and the blue expanse of the Atlantic Ocean.

27 centre right At 640 metres, Las Carboneras is one of the most charming and characteristic villages on the Anaga peninsula.

*27 bottom right The paths on the Anaga peninsula lead the trekker to the most interesting villages on Tenerife. These are the houses of Taborno with the Taganana mountains in the background.
Photographs by Stefano Ardito*

TOUBKAL AND ITS NEIGHBOURS

At the gateway to Marrakesh, the
ascent to the highest peaks of the Atlas

Magic, spectacular Marrakesh. The elegant lines of the large mosques, the minaret of Koutoubiya, the pavilions of the royal palace of El Badi, the great bustle of Djemaâ el Fna, the great triangular square on the edge of the souks with its traders, performers, stalls selling mint tea, shish kebab and all kinds of sweetmeats. Founded shortly after the year One Thousand, embellished and enriched by the sovereigns Almoravides and Almohades, Marrakesh has always been a cross-roads for the routes going towards the coast, mountains and desert: it is the most famous and popular city in Morocco. Deservedly so. In all seasons - but especially in winter and in early spring - the ancient capital has a special appearance, far different from that of Fez, Rabat and Meknès, the three other imperial cities in the country. The Upper Atlas mountains close the horizon to the south beyond the minarets, cupolas, old houses of the medina and the Andalusian-style walls and doors protecting the town. When the chain is clad with snow, the vision of this white, spectacular and gleaming barrier adds to the remarkable fascination.

If you imagine the Maghreb as a world of deserts, palms and oases alone, the great mountains of Morocco will be a surprise. If you do not like walking, even the winding roads leading to the high passes of Tizi-n-Tichka and Tizi-n-Test - retracing the great caravan routes of the past - afford views of rounded and severe peaks, harsh rocky valleys and villages flaunting their curious, turreted houses, with characteristic storks' nests often perched on roofs and chimneys. Wild and majestic, the Upper Atlas summits culminate in the 4,168 metres of Gebel Toubkal, the "roof of the Maghreb", and then in the 4,088 metres of Gebel Ouanoukrim, the 4,015 metres of Afella, the 4,010 metres

28-29 A lovely sweeping view over the village of Tinrorine, situated on the Toubkal massif, in the Upper Atlas. As can be seen the area is quite rich in water and marked by a lush vegetation. Photograph by Christope Boisvieux

of Akioud and the 3,974 metres of Tazaghart; the north eastern side of the latter possesses the highest and most spectacular faces of the entire chain. All these peaks close the deep valleys of Asif-n-Mizane and Asif Azzadene and are reached from the characteristic mountain resorts of Asni and Imlil. Slightly eastwards, yet more beautiful mountains (the most spectacular is Angour, 3,616 metres) crown the plateau and ski resort of Oukaimeden, the best known in Morocco. The overall extension of the Upper Atlas is enormous. Stretching for almost 400 kilometres between Tizi-n-Test and Midelt, the chain numbers hundreds of peaks rising above 3,000 metres and splendid rock faces such as those closing the magnificent Todhra canyon, isolated and wild massifs, such as Irghil M'Goun (4,068 metres) and Gebel Ayachi (3,737 metres) which marks the north-eastern extreme of the chain opposite the cedar forests and plateaus of the Middle Atlas. Of all, the Toubkal massif is by far the most popular and best known. Loved by hikers and mountaineers since the Twenties, it possesses a good network of refuge huts and expert, competent guides, this corner of the chain has more visitors than any other part of the Atlas and indeed of Morocco. Long, stony and scenic, the path climbing from the 1,750 metres of Imlil to the 3,200 metres of the refuge hut and the 4,168 metres of the peak every year sees thousands upon thousands of climbers anxious to reach the top: numbers that do not decrease in winter and in early spring when Toubkal and its neighbours become famous destinations for mountaineering-skiers from all over Europe. However interesting, a return journey from Imlil to Toubkal does not provide a complete picture of the valleys and highest peaks of the Atlas. In the vicinity, the number of possible treks is practically endless. We shall describe a trek lasting approximately a week: it is physically quite demanding and combines the ascent of Toubkal with that of Angour (3,616 metres), the graceful rocky peak closing the Oukaimeden depression to the south, and the Ouanoukrim (4,088 metres), the south-west neighbour of the highest summit; from here the view spreads farther towards the Sahara and the isolated Sirwa range. This allows optimum use of the Oukaimeden, Tacheddirt, Imlil, Toubkal (or Neltner) and Tazaghart (or Lépiney) refuge huts and camp equipment is not necessary. A series of variations can be made to reduce the physical demands of the route. The choice of period is also important. In the height of summer the paths are easy but the presence of long stretches of uncovered screes make some of the gorges on the route particularly exhausting. It is certainly preferable to tackle these mountains in late spring, when the snow covering the stony slopes allows a more enjoyable advancement. In this case, however, an ice-axe and crampons are needed and anyone wishing to use mules should check whether the route is accessible to these animals. In all cases, this easy adventure amidst the rocks and snows of Toubkal will encourage an early return to the mountains of Morocco. For winter lovers - snow permitting - we suggest the remarkable skiing options offered by the plateaux of the Middle Atlas. Those who prefer the colours of the stone and the culture of the Berber villages and mountain pastures should choose the preSahara Sirwa and Sarrho ranges. The next itinerary is dedicated to the first of these.

30 A Berber shepherd girl set against the contrasting colours of the whole region. Photograph by Christophe Boisvieux

31 top This Berber village stands near Gebel Sarrho, a short distance from the trekking area. Photograph by Marco Majrani

31 bottom In the remote Atlas mountain valleys the mule is still the most common and

convenient means of transport to isolated houses and villages. Photograph by Marco Majrani

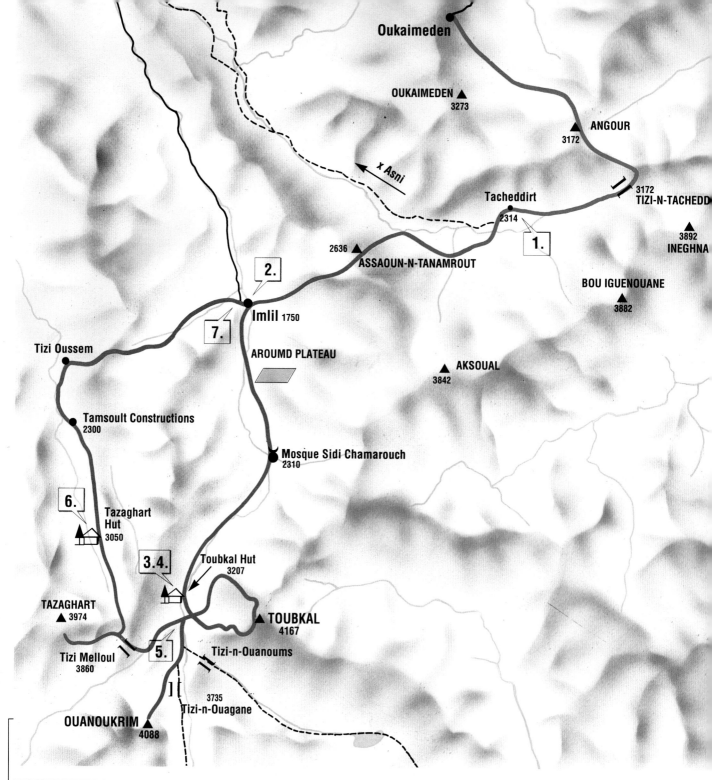

Oukaimeden

OUKAIMEDEN ▲
3273

▲ ANGOUR
3172

x Asni

Tacheddirt ▲ 3172
2314 TIZI-N-TACHEDD

1.

▲ 3892
INEGHNA

2636 ▲
ASSAOUN-N-TANAMROUT

BOU IGUENOUANE
▲ 3882

2.

Imlil 1750

7.

AROUMD PLATEAU

▲ AKSOUAL
3842

Tizi Oussem

Tamsoult Constructions
2300

● Mosque Sidi Chamarouch
2310

6.

Tazaghart
Hut
3050

3.4.

Toubkal Hut
3207

TAZAGHART
▲ 3974

▲ TOUBKAL
4167

Tizi Melloul
3860

5.

Tizi-n-Ouanoums

3735
Tizi-n-Ouagane

OUANOUKRIM ▲
4088

USEFUL INFORMATION

Duration: from 5 to 7 days. Only particularly well trained hikers can complete this itinerary without including one or two days' rest.
Elevation: from 1,740 to 4,168 metres.
Period: this route is in good condition for hikers from May to mid October. Until the end of June crampons and an ice-axe may be useful in some snow-covered gorges. In the height of summer

it is very hot. In winter and in early spring Toubkal and the peaks nearby are popular ski resorts.
Red tape: no visa is required for Morocco and no permits are necessary to visit the mountains.
Degree of difficulty: some easy (grade I) but exposed climbing passages are encountered in the ascent of the Angour. The steep snow-covered gorges in spring require care, especially at dawn when they may be icy.
Physical challenge: considerable if the route is covered without the inclusion of rest days. Beware of the heat in August!

Equipment: normal trekking gear at the height of summer. An ice-axe and crampons will be useful if these mountains are visited in late spring. Thanks to the refuge huts no tent is needed.
Access routes: the ski resort of Oukaimeden (2,620 metres) is reached along seventy-five kilometres of asphalt road from Marrakesh. Another good road runs between the main city and Imlil (1,750 metres). The return from Imlil can be made by bus; from Marrakesh to Oukaimeden you have to take a taxi.

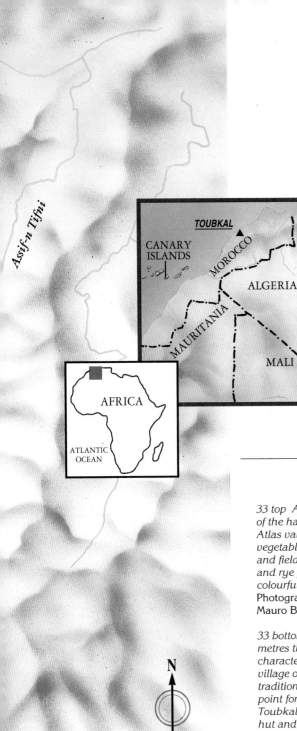

Asif-n Tifni

TOUBKAL

CANARY
ISLANDS

MOROCCO

ALGERIA

MAURITANIA

MALI

AFRICA

ATLANTIC
OCEAN

N

33 top At the foot of the harsh, barren Atlas valleys, vegetable gardens and fields of barley and rye produce a colourful mosaic. Photograph by Mauro Burzio

33 bottom At 1750 metres the characteristic Berber village of Imlil is the traditional starting point for the Toubkal (or Neltner) hut and the highest peaks in Morocco. Photograph by Marco Majrani

Guides and porters: guides and beasts of burden can be hired at the Oukaimeden and Imlil offices.

Detours and peaks: Angour (3,614 metres), Toubkal (4,168 metres), Ouanoukrim (4,088 metres) and the impressive but easy Tazaghart (3,974 metres) are on the basic trek proposed. Numerous other peaks can be added to the route starting with the easy Akioud (4,010 metres). Of these, the lovely rocky needle of Tadat (3,760 metres) is for climbers.

In case of trouble: the huts are manned, equipped with first aid material and stretchers and can be reached by mules. On the edges of the massif problems can be more serious: travelling with one or more mules simplifies matters in case of accidents.

Maps: the best is the Oukaimeden - Toubkal sheet of the 1/100,000 Carte du Maroc.

Guidebooks: there are no guides in Italian on the mountains of Morocco. Available in French are *Le Haut Atlas* by André Fougerolles (Glénat, 1991) and *Le Maroc - Les plus belles courses et randonnées* by Bernard Domenech (Denoel, 1989). In English *Atlas Mountains - Morocco* by Robin G. Collomb (West Col.

1980). To learn more of the country we recommend *Marocco* by Touring Club Italiano (1994) and *Maroc* in the famous Guides Bleus series (Hachette, 1981).

For further reading: there are a great many books on Morocco but only rarely are they on the Atlas. Besides the works of Tahar Ben Jelloun, Pierre Loti and Paul Bowles (the film *The sheltering sky* was based on his book of the same title) we recommend *I berberi marocchini* by A. Koller (Tell, 1952) and *Maroc - Faune et grands espaces* by D. Briand (1992).

FIRST DAY

from Oukaimeden
to Angour and Tacheddirt
distance climbed: 1,000 metres
distance descended: 1,300 metres
time: 7 hours 30 minutes

The trek commences with a long, exhausting stage and with certain exposed parts in the ascent to the elegant Angour peak. Those wishing a more gentle start can follow the easy mule path crossing the Tizi-n-Wadi (2,918 metres), used in both cases by the mules. Leave the ski resort of Oukaimeden and follow a dirt track for a while (if you go by car you will save an hour). Proceed along the valley leading to Angour and climb steeply to Tizi-n-Itbir (3,295 metres). Continue along a wide gravel gorge to the right of a rocky spur; pass a col and proceed along narrow rather exposed ledges to the top plateau. An easy climb leads to the summit (3,616 metres). Another path follows the wide east ridge, before descending on narrow ledges to Tizi-n-Tacheddirt (3,172 metres). A very long series of turns at the foot of the south face of Angour then a wide valley lead to Tacheddirt (2,314 metres).

SECOND DAY

from Tacheddirt to Imlil
distance climbed: 400 metres
distance descended: 850 metres
time: 5 hours

A short, easy stage, all on a dirt track and permitting some rest after the rough, tiring hike to the Angour peak. The route, fairly monotonous but of scenic interest, should be completed by reaching the nearby and easy panoramic spot of Assaoun-n-Tanamrout. Start by descending to ford the river, leaving a dirt track to Asni to the right, and climb up again crossing a number of other streams to the unnamed saddle (2,259 metres); from here a lovely detour (2 hours return) leads to Assaoun-n-Tanamrout (2,636 metres). Back at the pass, descend into a gorge and pass a village down to Imlil (1,750 metres).

34 top On the paths of the Upper Atlas mules are indispensable companions on the trekker's adventure. This is on the path to Toubkal, above Sidi Chamarouch. Photograph by Marco Majrani

34 centre A party of trekkers climbing the stony bends of the path from Imlil to Toubkal, just below the village of Sidi Chamarouch. Photograph by Marco Majrani

34 bottom A tier of terraces patiently irrigated and cultivated with wheat, barley and corn rises towards the Berber village of Imlil, the starting point of ascents to Toubkal. Photograph by Marco Majrani

THIRD DAY

from Imlil
to the Toubkal (or Neltner) Hut
distance climbed: 1,550 metres
time: 4 hours 30 minutes

Not a particularly tiring day, devoted to the busiest path of the Upper Atlas, leading to the foot of Toubkal and other peaks that encircle it. The path starts amid the fields of maize, leaving to the right the path for the Tazaghart Hut, and climbs steeply to the Aroumd plateau. After a stretch on the flat, another climb leads to the sparse houses and mosque of Sidi Chamarouch (2,310 metres). Continue over a steep drop in the valley, crossing a deep morainic hollow and cross a marshy area to the refuge hut (3,207 metres).

FOURTH DAY

from the Toubkal (or Neltner) Hut
to Gebel Toubkal and back
distance climbed: 950 metres
distance descended: 950 metres
time: 6 hours 30 minutes

Not particularly long but certainly tiring because of the altitude and the deadly screes on the final stretch, the path to the Toubkal peak deserves to be trod with the first snow. The view from the summit is, nonetheless, always splendid in all directions. After crossing the river, climb in the southern Irhzer-n-Ikhibi hollow, which gradually becomes steeper and more tiring, decidedly more pleasant if covered in snow. Leave this to the left on easy rocks and

35 top Two trekkers
on the nromal route
up Gebel Toubkal,
above the most tiring
stretch. Behind them
the majestic
Tazaghart peak rises
to 3974 metres.
Photograph by
Stefano Ardito

cross the morainic terrace that concludes with Tizi-n-Toubkal. Move left again and you will come to more tiring gravel slopes. It is best to move crosswise to the right and reach the ridge leading to the summit (4,167 metres) as quickly as possible. The descent is quick and without problems. It is also possible to climb via another hollow, farther north (left looking from the hut) where the snow lies for longer than on the normal route. Expert and well-equipped mountaineers can climb the panoramic Ouanoums and Ifni ridges (both AD with IV passages).

FIFTH DAY
from the Toubkal
(or Neltner) Refuge Hut
to Gebel Ouanoukrim and back
distance climbed: 880 metres
distance descended: 880 metres
time: 5 hours 30 minutes

The collection of the great summits of the Atlas cannot be complete without Gebel Ouaounoukrim, simpler and less tiring than Toubkal. From the refuge hut follow the bottom of the valley towards Tizi-n-Ouanoums to a plateau, from where you climb up a wide gorge of gravel or snow to the saddle of Tizi-n-Ouagane (3,735 metres). Continue on the beautiful and easy ridge to a rock marker, move to the right then return to the edge following it to the summit (4,088 metres). Descend by the same route. Ouanoukrim offers various more demanding ridge climbs.

SIXTH DAY
from Toubkal (or Neltner) Hut
to Tazaghart and Tazaghart
(or Lépiney) Hut
distance climbed: 800 metres
distance descended: 960 metres
time: 7 hours

Leaving the crowds of the normal route and the Toubkal Hut behind you, plunge into the wildest and most spectacular part of the chain, quite exposed between the two hills and close to the Tazaghart summit. The ascent to Tizi-n-Amharas-n-Iglioua is rather steep. Climb up for a while towards Tizi-n-Ouanoums, then take and follow a deep ravine; beyond this a stretch crossways leads to Tizi-n-Amharas-n-Iglioua (3,815 metres). From here you can climb quickly to the Akioud peak (4,010 metres, 1 hour 15 minutes return). A crossing on awkward and rocky terrain leads to Tizi Melloul (3,860 metres) and the start of the easy ridge of the normal route up Tazaghart (3,974 metres). Back at the pass, descend along the steep stony or snow-clad slopes into the cirque of Arhzane and continue in a deep ravine dominated by the Tazaghart rock faces to the refuge hut of the same name (3,050 metres).

SEVENTH DAY
from Tazaghart (or Lépiney) Hut
to Imlil
distance climbed: 250 metres
distance descended: 1,550 metres
time: 5 hours

The final day of the trek follows the easy but long path to the refuge hut, most of which amid junipers. Descend with a few short climbs to the Tamsoult structures (2,300 metres, there is a small refuge hut). Descend again briefly towards Tizi Oussem, then leave the bottom of the valley and climb to the right (east) to the saddle of Tizi-n-Tacht (2,489 metres). A good mule path descends amidst pasture land and sparse woods to Imlil.

35 centre top
A comfortable
construction,
erected between
the two world wars,
the Neltner hut,
also known as
the Toubkal Hut,
stands at 3207
metres. Visible in
the background
are the awkward
and tiring stretches
of gravel found
on the first part
of the climb and
approach to
Toubkal.
Photograph by
Marco Majrani

35 centre bottom
The last slope before
the Toubkal peak
is the most exhausting
of the whole ascent.
To the right some
trekkers pass the rocks
on the eastern slope.
Photograph by
Marco Majrani

35 bottom A metal
pyramid indicates the
4,167 metres of the
Gebel Toubkal peak.
The great Sahara
stretches out in the
background, beyond
the Sirwa massif.
Photograph by
Marco Majrani

THE GEBEL SIRWA CIRCUIT

A fascinating trek on the edge of the
Moroccan Sahara

Sheer rocks, harsh stony plateaux, valleys that are suddenly tinged with green. A little south of the High Atlas, within sight of Toubkal and the other highest peaks in the country but already overlooking the vast mineral expanses of the Sahara, Gebel Sirwa shows visitors the other side of the Moroccan mountains. A mineral world even harsher and more impressive than the "four thousand" to the south of Marrakesh and where you can still spot antelopes, vultures and with a little more luck the serval, the large mountain wildcat of the Sahara.

Most of all, there is a mountain range unknown to mass tourism, where the customs are still those of the past, traditions are still very much alive, the villages have splendid unfired clay buildings and the people are smiling and friendly.

Isolated, surrounded by splendid solitary valleys, Gebel Sirwa is perhaps the least known mountain in Morocco. It is an extinct volcano rising to 3,305 metres and marks the southernmost point of the Atlas before the vast Sahara. The starting point for the mountain is the town of Ouarzazate, one of the places where Morocco is experiencing the most rapid change. In less than ten years the sleepy town on the edge of the desert - a military garrison, a camping site, a couple of hotels - has turned into a large tourist resort with four and five star hotels, an airport with direct flights to Europe and crowds of visitors in the streets.

A few kilometres away there are film sets and open air studios used by film crews from all over the world.

Just an hour's drive off the good road between Ouarzazate and the Agadir coast and you are in a very different world. All the villages at the foot of the Sirwa massif (the most important are Tagouyamt, Atougha and Ti-n-Iddr) have splendid unfired clay buildings and have conserved the sturdy, fortified barns built in the past to defend the village food reserves from marauders. The valleys are barren and rocky but contain precious patches of pastureland. Above two thousand metres, the pastures become villages true and proper where the herdsmen's families live from June to September every year.

36-37 Some trekkers head for the Gebel Sirwa that dominates the landscape between Ouarzazate and the Upper Atlas. Photograph by Stefano Ardito

37 The Tagouyamt mosque is the starting point of the trek. In the background are the bare slopes of Gebel Sirwa. Photograph by Stefano Ardito

At the end of the annual transhumance, the head of each family climbs to the top of the highest peak on Sirwa to sacrifice a sheep: the mountain has always been venerated by the local peoples as a beneficial source of water and of wealth. As on all the desert chains, the winter is icy and the summer scorching. The spring, fleeting but wonderful, offers the weather conditions for hiking and splendid flowers in bloom.

For the trekker, Sirwa is a magnificent ground for easy and interesting adventures. In two days you can go

stopping places and encouraging the growth of small, local tourist agencies specialized in this type of activity. The "Grande Traversée des Atlas Marocains" based on the French "Grande Traversée des Alpes" covers four mountains (Sirwa, Sarrho, Toubkal and Mgoun) and more than 50 villages.

Over seven years, the courses held in the Tabannt Training Centre (which also produces agricultural experts, artisans, builders skilled in the traditional methods of the Atlas) have qualified 153 mountain escorts; approx. 80% of these manage to

from Tagouyamt or from Ti-n-Iddr to the highest peak and back, in four or five you can cross the peak and go all the way round the massif, passing isolated valleys and high altitude pastures, bizarre rock formations and unexpected lakes. On Sirwa, for some years now, the paths have become part of an important network. With the aid of French state cooperation, in seven years (between 1985 and 1992) lots of money has been spent training guides, equipping

make a living this way and many are specialized in rock climbing, mountain skiing or canyon descents. Small but inviting stopping places have been created in the villages, mainly for trekkers but also capable of accommodating other visitors to the area. They are often in the most characteristic and oldest buildings; some are run privately but most by the local community. Other mountain dwellers supplement their incomes as farmers and herdsmen by working as

mule or car drivers or selling the carpets that are made at home by the women. This short and easy hike on Sirwa can be combined with a visit to the other mountains in Morocco - in particular the nearby Toubkal - or a stop in the desert in the direction of Zagora or the splendid dunes of Erfoud, or a visit to the fascinating Marrakesh. In spring, the most suitable season for a trek on the massif, a seaside stopover can be scheduled on the coast of Agadir!

38 The Merzouga dunes, a short distance from Erfoud, are the most spectacular and frequently photographed in the Moroccan Sahara.

38-39 After a visit to Gebel Sirwa a trip should be made into the desert, towards the lovely area of Erfoud where sandy dunes and rock formations alternate to create a beautiful landscape.
Photographs by Marie Anne Chamel/ Agence Freestyle

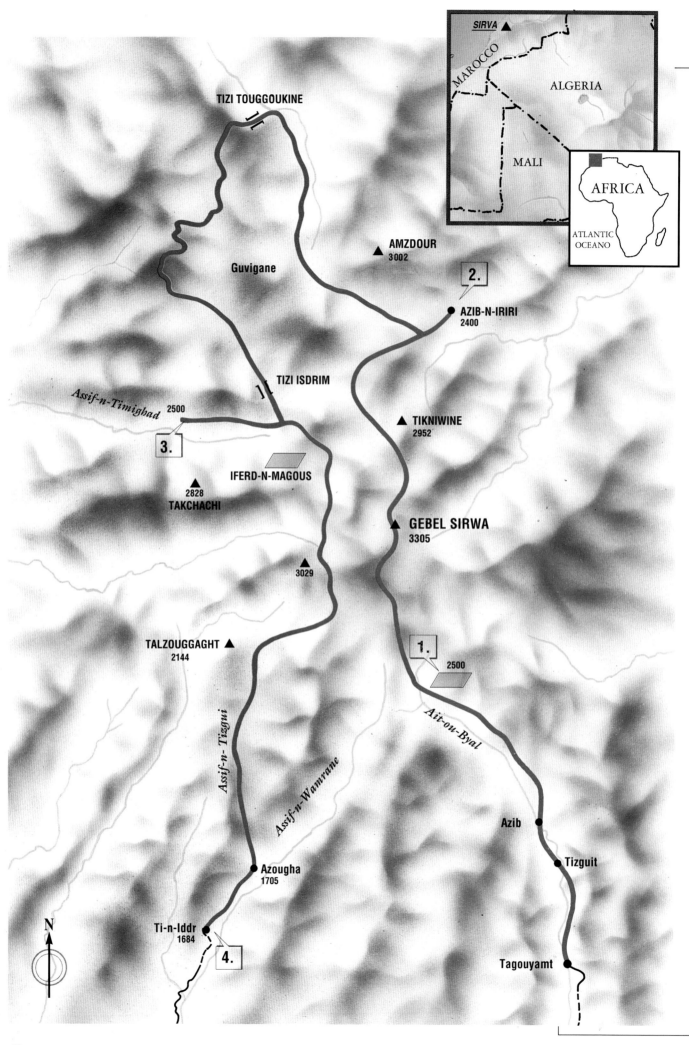

USEFUL INFORMATION

Duration: 4 days.
Elevation: from 1,684 to 3,308 metres.
Period: the best seasons are the middle ones, spring being recommended for the flowers. The summer is truly very hot.
Red tape: no visa is required for Morocco, nor are any permits required for trips into the mountains.
Degree of difficulty: the trek is all along paths that present no problems. The exception is the ascent to the rocky peak of Sirwa as this includes short but aerial 2nd degree passages both on ascent and descent.
Physical challenge: average. But be careful in summer!
Equipment: normal trekking gear. A tent and cooking material are necessary only if you decide to hike without assistance. A 20 metres rope is useful to secure the less expert during the ascent and descent of the peak.
Access routes: Ouarzazate is approx. 150 kilometres from the Assif-ou-Byal and Assif-n-Wamrane valleys and the lovely villages of Ti-n-Iddr (1,684 metres), Atougha (1,705 metres) and Tagouyamt (1,950 metres), first on asphalt and then on trails usually presenting no problems. A short detour to the beautiful rock pinnacles of Taslit is recommended.
Guides and porters: a guide can be hired directly in the villages around Sirwa or assistance can be obtained in one of the numerous agencies in Marrakesh, Casablanca or Rabat specialized in trekking and adventure trips.
Detours and peaks: the Sirwa peak (3,305 metres) is on the basic trek. Short and easy detours lead to Talzouggaght (2,844 metres) and Amzdour (3,002 metres). The two elegant twin peaks of the Tikiniwine (2,907 and 2,952 metres) are reached via not simple rock climbs.
In case of trouble: the trails and dirt tracks around the mountain permit a fairly rapid evacuation of any injured; if the group has mules the matter is even easier.

Maps: the best is the *Taliwine* sheet of the *Carte du Maroc* 1:100 000.
Guidebooks: the guides on the Moroccan mountains contain only brief details regarding Sirwa. The two excellent brochures *Maroc - montagnes et vallées* and *La Grande Traversée des Atlas Marocains* can be obtained from the National Tourist Board of Morocco or directly from the Centre d'Information sur la montagne - c/o Ministère du Tourisme, 1 Rue d'Oujda, Rabat, tel. (00212)(7)701280, fax 760915.

41 top The road that from Ouarzazate leads to Zagora and the Sahara runs along several fortified ksour. Photograph by Marco Majrani

41 bottom The picturesque village of Ti-n-Iddr, linked to Ouarzazate by a trail in quite good condition, marks the end of the trek. Photograph by Stefano Ardito

FIRST DAY
from Tagouyamt
to the Ait-ou-Byal valley
distance climbed: 700 metres
time: 3 hours 30 minutes

42 top A party of trekkers camps among the houses of Tagouyamt (1,950 metres) before starting off for Sirwa.

42 centre top Making camp in a beautiful clearing at 2,500 metres in the upper Ait-ou-Byal valley at the end of the first day.

42 centre bottom A caravan of mules carrying provisions and baggage follows a party of hikers on the path climbing the Ait-ou-Byal vallley from the village of Azib.

42 bottom A long break on the second leg of the trek between the Ait-ou-Byal valley and the pens just under the Sirwa peak.

A short and easy stage that constitutes an approach to the high mountain world. There are beautiful, fortified barns in the rocky gorge preceding Tizguit. From Tagouyamt start up with a wide mule-track across the mountain; this leads in approximately one hour to the foot of the rocky gorge and the fortified barns. A series of turns will take you to the houses of Azib from where you proceed along a wide ridge and then crossways on the mountain to enter the upper part of the Ait-ou-Bayal valley. Camp in a lovely clearing at 2,500 metres, within sight of a waterfall.

SECOND DAY
from the Ait-ou-Byal Valley
to Gebel Sirwa and Azib-n-Iriri
distance climbed: 850 metres
distance descended: 950 metres
time: 7 hours

A long and tiring stage but one of great interest, leading to the highest peak on the range and then to the pastures and stone constructions of Azib-n-Iriri, within sight of the rocky summits of Tikniwine. Go along the valley to its head, turn right beside some rocky pinnacles and climb a monotonous slope to some pens. Climb for a stretch across the mountain then up a ravine to the base of the Sirwa summit, a hundred metres high. Approach it along a crevice, go right on an exposed ledge (2nd degree), and a second crevice will lead you out of difficulty. An easy aerial ridge (1st degree passages) reaches the summit (3,305 metres). Descend on the other side along sheet rock and crevices, another climbing section (2nd degree crevice) and proceed on easy ground beside a deep and steep canal. At the end of this, descend to the left into a valley and follow it for quite a while, skirting Tikniwine from the north, until you reach Azib-n-Iriri (2,400 metres).

THIRD DAY

from Azib-n-Iriri to Assif-n-Timighad
distance climbed: 850 metres
distance descended: 750 metres
time: 6 hours

A long day of zigzags on which you will emerge onto the plateau north of Sirwa within sight of Toubkal. Start with a steep and monotonous climb - the base of the Amzdour rocks - to a wide stony ridge (2,800 metres). Cross on the other side and a stony valley leads to the bottom of a group of lovely,

rocky pinnacles to be skirted (2,400 metres approx.) on a dirt track. Four kilometres along the road you will reach a wide grassy valley that rises towards the Tizi Isdrim pass (2,850 metres); from here it descends in the green Assif-n-Timighad valley to an attractive, grassy hollow, ideal for camping (2,500 metres approx.).

FOURTH DAY

from Assi-n-Timighad to Ti-n-Iddr
distance climbed: 300 metres
distance descended: 1,110 metres
time: 5 hours 30 minutes

Highly varied and interesting, the final stage of the trek leads to a group of very charming villages. Start by climbing to the marshy plateau of Iferd-n-Magous, an excellent scenic spot on the western side of Sirwa. From a first pass between Taiçda and Sirwa climb across the mountain to a rocky

panoramic ridge (3,029 metres) from where you descend to the right (west) on the plateau at the foot of Talzouggaght, in an area much eroded and full of rocky pinnacles. Go down into the wide Assif-n-Tizgui valley, overlooking Assif-n-Wamrane and its villages from above, and then descend with steep turns to Azougha (1,705 metres). Once across the village you will soon reach Ti-n-Idder (1,684 metres).

43 left A colourful carpet of flowers accompanies the crossing of the marshy Iferd-n-Magous plateau on the fourth leg of the trek.

43 top right Once the most difficult passages have been overcome, a scenic ridge zigzags to the top of Sirwa at 3305 metres.

43 centre After a number of steep turns the trek reaches the characteristic houses of Azougha (1705 metres), the highest village in the Assif-n-Wamrane valley.

43 bottom Ti-n-Iddr (1684 metres). This village marks the end of the trek, showing the visitor its characteristic earthen buildings. The houses of Azougha appear in the background.
Photographs by
Stefano Ardito

THE PEAKS OF THE HOGGAR AND TEFEDEST

On the "Dolomites"
of the Algerian Sahara

44 left
The traditional blue or azure chèch *knotted on the head with a complicated ritual is still used every day by the Tuareg who live in the Algerian Sahara.*

44 right The eyes of the Tuareg below the chèch *seem to scrutinize the sweeping desert horizon.*

45 A Tuareg and his camel follow a path in the rocky desert at the foot of the Hoggar mountains.
Photographs by
Anne Conway

"A large blue bus is waiting in the middle of a street in Algiers. In front of it are a dozen or so passengers, on its sides the stops along its interminable journey are written in black letters." It was 2 April 1935 and what seems the beginning of an adventure story is the first step - 3,000 kilometres from the rocks - towards mountaineering in the Sahara. On that bus, together with

olive tree grows. Then they came out onto the plateau.

"We are navigating in the middle of Atlantis on the most monstrous vessel that our imagination could have invented" wrote Frison-Roche in his *Carnets Sahariens*.

In the heart of the Sahara, in the southernmost corner of Algeria, the fantastic granite peaks of the Hoggar and the nearby Tefedest

captain Raymond Coche and count Chasseloup-Laubat was Roger Frison-Roche, a guide from Chamonix, author of some of the best selling mountain books of all times.

The group were headed for the most famous and feared mountain in the Sahara, Garet el-Djenoun standing in the heart of the Tefedest range, in the extreme south of Algeria.

For the Tuareg this is the "moutain of the spirits", a presence to be kept at a distance. Two weeks later, in the cool morning air Frison-Roche and Captain Coche tackled the last difficult passages: an exposed chimney, a stretch of crumbling rock, a narrow ledge where a wild

have for sixty years been a clear challenge for mountaineers the world over. With their rough rocks, giddy crests, fissures rounded by the incessant desert wind, the pinnacles of these mountains - Garet el-Djenoun, Tahoulag, Saouinan, Tizouyadj - offer challenges of an extraordinary grace in one of the loveliest environments of Africa and indeed of all the mountains in the world.

There is no shortage of peaks that can be reached by the hiker without particular difficulty, starting with Tahat, at 2,918 metres the highest point in Algeria. There are also plenty of opportunities for those who prefer a *méharée*, a hike with the

back-up of a caravan of camels; in this way even the traveller just off the plane can experience the emotions of the merchants who, for thousands of years, have crossed the largest desert on earth. On Tefedest other paths on more rocky ground lead to interesting sites of cave drawing not unlike the far more famous ones of Tassili.

The most interesting place, Mertoutek, was discovered in 1935 by Roger Frison-Roche and lies a few kilometres north of the village of the same name. Other drawings can be admired, in particular at Tan Tfeltasin, Tankobrane, Tan Ainesnis and Ouan Tanout. The trek in search of the most interesting sites on

it is a wonder. It is impossible to see it and not think of God" he wrote in the hermitage where he was killed in 1916 by a group of rebel Libyans.

Over the past sixty years the ranges in this part of Algeria (in particular the Hoggar, the most spectacular and most easily reached from Tamanrasset) have become one of the most popular destinations in Africa for European travellers in search of the distant horizons and extraordinary atmosphere of the desert. Particularly popular is the Atakor chain, the most spectacular in the area that comprises several of the more graceful peaks.

Tefedest takes two or three days. Long before archaeologists and mountaineers came to these rocks, an extraordinary European lived among the peaks. Born in 1858 in Strasbourg, father Charles-Eugène de Foucauld visited the Sahara in 1883-84 with a military expedition. After leaving the army he chose to follow the church and retreated in prayer in 1905 to a hermitage built on the Assekrem. "The view is lovelier than can be imagined. Nothing can convey the idea of the mass of peaks and rocky pinnacles at your feet:

As for the not distant Tassili - the seven hundred kilometres of trail separating Tamanrasset from Djanet are no distance compared with the immensity of the Sahara! - the serious clashes that have lacerated Algeria since early 1992 have at the time of writing made these places of extraordinary beauty off-limits for all foreign visitors. Algeria will hopefully soon return to peace so that the magnificent summits of the Sahara may once more become a possible destination for all.

Not only the rocks and dunes are

of interest in this remarkable land. Close to Tamanrasset it is possible to visit Tuareg camps (singular is Targui); these are one of the most unusual and fascinating peoples in Africa.

Converted to Islam around the year One Thousand and eternal nomads, these men and women speak a Berber tongue (Tamahaq) with a strange hissing sound and amaze those who meet them with their costumes, their character and the pride that stems from thousands of years spent in one of the harshest environments on earth.

46 left A hiker heads for the great smooth round rocks of Tesnou set amid spectacular sandy dunes.
Photograph by Mario Verin

47 bottom A Tuareg cuts firewood near one of the villages at the foot of the Hoggar.
Photograph by Anne Conway

USEFUL INFORMATION

Duration: we describe a series of day climbs to be made over a period of 7-10 days.

Elevation: from the 1,395 metres of Tamanrasset to the 2,918 of Tahat.

Period: all year round but the middle seasons are recommended. The summer is truly scorching and in winter the temperature can fall to minus 10° centigrade.

Red tape: a visa is required for Algeria. No special permits are needed for trekking.

Degree of difficulty: these are mountain ascents and any non-experts should be accompanied and secured to a guide. The Hoggar and Tefedest ranges include numerous easily accessible minor peaks such as Assekrem (2,728 metres) quickly reached from the Assekrem refuge hut and father De Foucauld's hermitage.

Physical challenge: average for the Tefedest peaks, average-low for the Hoggar.

Equipment: for the peaks described climbing equipment with ropes, cords, snaplinks, chocks, helmet and descender is useful.

Access routes: Tamanrasset (1,395 metres), the town at the base of the range and the crossroads of southern Algeria, is connected by daily flights from Algiers. The trip overland is 1,920 kilometres from Algiers and 2,400 from Tunis. From Tamanrasset, a steep dirt track runs in a 185 kilometres ring around the Hoggar: approximately halfway along the trek is the Col de l'Assekrem. Mertoutek, the village at the base of the Tefedest peaks is reached by returning north on the road for In Salah and turning right on a track that starts just past Im Amguel (230 kilometres from Tamanrasset to Mertoutek).

Guides and porters: inside the Hoggar National Park it is obligatory to be accompanied by a guide although he will be lacking in specialist mountaineering training. On both the massifs baggage travels on dromedary or mule-back.

Detours and peaks: in the Hoggar and Tefedest ranges numerous other

48 top For a visit to the Hoggar peaks an alternative to 4X4 wheels is a meharée, a hike on which the baggage is carried by camels. Photograph by Didier Givois

48 bottom The presence of bizarre rock forms turns the mountains of the Sahara into true open air geological museums. The picture shows the blocks of basaltic rock sculpted by the wind on Amezzouroug, a spectacular peak in the Hoggar range. Photograph by Anne Conway

peaks (including Hadriane, llamane and, of course, Assekrem) can be reached with no great difficulty. There are hundreds of treks for expert climbers. The trek from Tamanrasset to the foot of Assekrem is relatively busy though not of exceptional interest and takes 5-6 days. There are numerous possible treks in the Tefedest range, in search of cave drawings similar to those of Tassili.

In case of trouble: should an accident occur, hikers and mountaineers must be able to redescend by their own means to the trails. There are no problems for 4x4 transport to Tamanrasset.

Maps: the treks described are shown in the sheets *Assekrem, Garet el-Djenoun* and *I-n-Ekker* of the *Carte du Sahara* 1:200 000 of the Algerian Institut National de Cartographie.

Guidebooks: information for hikers and mountaineers can be found in *Le Hoggar* by Claude Blanguernon

(Arthaud, 1973). General information on the area is contained in *Sahara - Guida al deserto* by B. Vaes, G. del Marmol and A. d'Otreppe (Edizioni Futuro, 1987). Also useful are the Guide Bleu *Algérie* (Hachette, 1986) and *Algeria* by Paolo Santacroce (Clup, 1980).

For further reading: details on the nature and mountaineering history is contained in *Uomini e montagne del Sahara* and in *Tuareg, Tassili, Sahara*, both by Mario Fantin (Tamari) and in *Hommes des Montagnes du Hoggar* by Odette Bernezat (Les Quatre seigneurs, 1975). Also interesting are *Le Lettere dal Sahara* by Alberto Moravia (Bompiani, 1981), *Terra degli Uomini* by Antoine de Saint-Exupéry (Garzanti, 1974). Information on the cave drawings of the Hoggar and Tefedest can be obtained from *Antiche civiltà del Sahara* by Massimo Baistrocchi (Mursia, 1986).

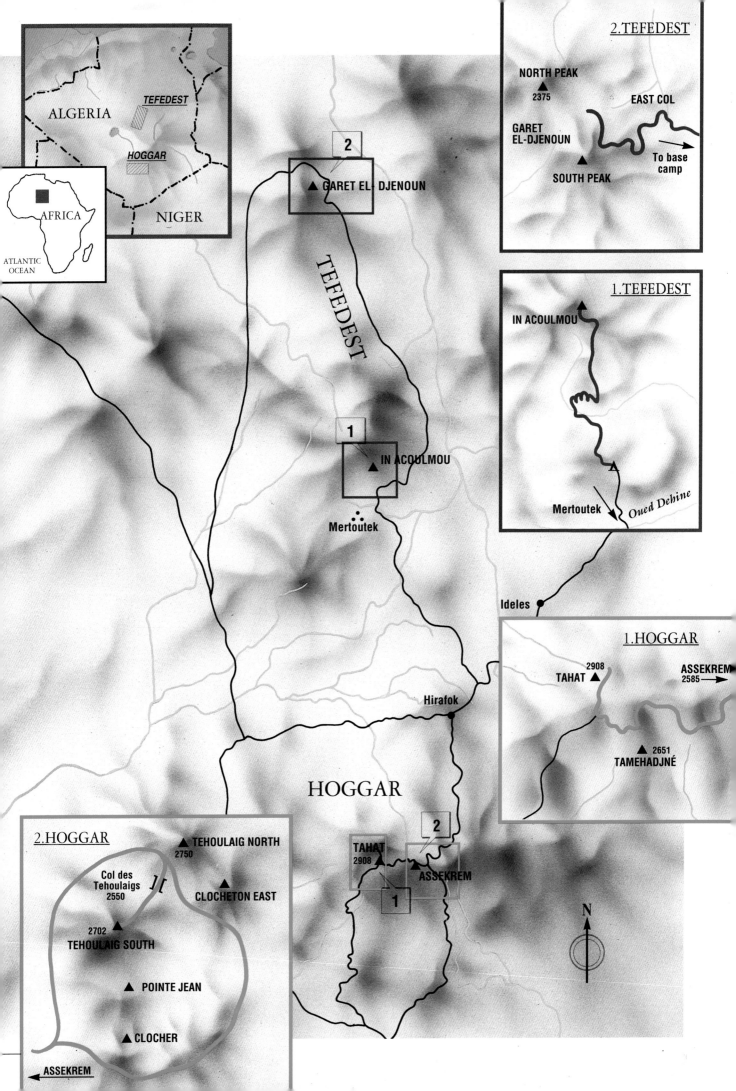

ALGERIA

TEFEDEST

HOGGAR

NIGER

AFRICA

ATLANTIC
OCEAN

2.TEFEDEST

NORTH PEAK
▲
2375

GARET
EL-DJENOUN

EAST COL

▲
SOUTH PEAK

To base
camp

2

▲ GARET EL-DJENOUN

T
E
F
E
D
E
S
T

1

▲ IN ACOULMOU

Mertoutek

1.TEFEDEST

IN ACOULMOU ▲

△

Mertoutek

Oued Dehine

Ideles

1.HOGGAR

TAHAT ▲ 2908

ASSEKREM
2585 →

▲ 2651
TAMEHADJNÉ

Hirafok

HOGGAR

2

TAHAT
2908
▲

▲
ASSEKREM

1

N

2.HOGGAR

▲ TEHOULAIG NORTH
2750

Col des
Tehoulaigs
2550

][

▲
CLOCHETON EAST

2702 ▲
TEHOULAIG SOUTH

▲ POINTE JEAN

▲ CLOCHER

← ASSEKREM

THE HOGGAR

FIRST DAY

from the Assekrem trail to Tahat
distance climbed: 750 metres
time: 7 hours

High and scenic but easily reached the Tahat summit (2,908 metres) is the highest of the Hoggar and all Algeria. A shapeless mound of rocks and stones it does not offer the traveller the graceful forms of many other pinnacles in the area. On the other hand, from this summit accessible to all hikers, the view sweeps over the peaks of Atakor and the great desert expanses to the north, beyond which appears the silhouette of the Tefedest range. From the Col de l'Assekrem follow the track westwards, as far as one of the two forks (respectively 10 and 15 kilometres) from which the secondary trails head northwards towards Tahat, in an area rich in prehistoric sites. Where the trails terminate (2,300 metres approximately) proceed on foot towards the clearly visible Tahat, climbing it on the wide and easy south side. It will take approximately 4 hours to reach the top (2,908 metres) and about 3 hours for the descent and return to the vehicle.

SECOND DAY

from the Assekrem trail
to Tehoulaig South
distance climbed: 350-500 metres
time: 3 - 4 hours 30 minutes

With its splendid organ pipe walls, sharp crests and sheets of compact volcanic rock, the Tehoulaig peak is the most refined and popular of Atakor and the whole Hoggar range. A stone's throw from the Assekrem trail, it has two principal peaks (Tehoulaig North and South, respectively 2,750 and 2,702 metres) flanked by various secondary peaks and pinnacles. All the routes to the northern peak are at least 4th degree, but the southern one is accessible to all hikers capable of managing 1st and 2nd degree passages. The complete tour of the mountain presents no difficulties. From the Col de l'Assekrem proceed for 6 kilometres to the beginning of the trail to Hirafok and Idelès. Park a little farther on (2,337 metres) and head on foot towards the impressive walls of the massif. Once at the base of the spectacular north-west face of Tehoulaig South - the loveliest of

51 left Sunset over the Hoggar mountains seen from the Assekrem is one of the most charming sights of all the African mountains.
Photograph by Anne Conway

*51 top right.
A caravan of camels follows the trail up to the Assekrem and father de Foucauld's hermitage.*
Photograph by Gudrun Bergdhal/ Agence Freestyle

*51 centre right
A maze of towers and rocky aiguilles dominates the trail up Assekrem in the heart of the Hoggar mountains.*
Photograph by Vincenzo Martegani

*51 bottom right
A double rope descent on the normal Ilamane route, a way first taken in 1935 by the Swiss Hermann Bossard and Walter Hauser.*
Photograph by Gudrun Bergdhal/ Agence Freestyle

the whole Hoggar! - go round it and then climb to the Col des Tehoulaigs (2,550 metres). Here starts the graceful and easy north east ridge of Tehoulaig South, to be followed along the sheets of rock and chimneys (1st and 2nd degree, mounds) to the 2,702 metres of the summit. Back at the pass descend south-eastwards and pass at the base of Tehoulaig North and Clocheton East before bearing right and returning to the starting point skirting a secondary rocky belt.
It takes three hours to finish the circle, plus 1 hour 30 minutes for the return journey to the peak.
It is also possible to go all the way round Tehoulaig North (1 hour extra).

TEFEDEST

52 left *The splendid grade two stone slabs on the upper section of the climb to In Acoulmou are the most interesting part of the ascent but special care must be taken on the way down.*

52 right top
A hiker crosses over a natural arch not far from the In Acoulmou peak.

52 centre right
Flat sheets of granite levelled by the desert wind have to be crossed at the foot of In Acoulmou but they are not particularly difficult.

52 bottom
An upward view reveals the weak points of In Acoulmou. As for many other peaks in the Sahara, the normal route up this mountains climbs zig zag, using the easiest passages.

53 An unmistakable monolithic ledge provides access to the highest part of the normal route up In Acoulmou (2,336 metres), one of the loveliest and most elegant peaks in the Tefedest range.
Photographs by Mario Verin

FIRST DAY
from Oued Dehine
to In Acoulmou and back
distance climbed: 600 metres
time: 8 hours

With its great and impressive horizontal sheets of granite, In Acoulmou is one of the most interesting and spectacular peaks of the Tefedest range. Not technically difficult, the mountain requires care

on the steep sheets of rock: the less expert must be secured with a rope! From Mertoutek, go to Oued Dehine and cross it heading north towards a wide valley. Camp at the base and the next day follow the valley to a pass; descend on the other side to a wide ridge and then climb up it again along easy sheets of rock. A long stretch across to the left leads to a plateau at the foot of the peak. You will come to a narrow ledge; skirt a tower and proceed along exposed but easy sheets of rock (1st and 2nd degree) to the peak (2,336 metres). On descent the sheets of rock on the upper section require care. The rest is easy.

54-55 *Numerous graffiti-decorated rocks can be visited near the small village of Mertoutek.*

54 bottom left
A trekker stops at the base of the steep ravine of blocks that leads to the normal route up Garet el-Djenoun (2,375 metres).
Photograph by Mario Verin

54 bottom right
The normal route up Garet el-Djenoun includes numerous crossings on smooth granite that require care and a sure foot.
Photograph by Mario Verin

SECOND DAY
from Oued Ti-n-Ekert
to Garet el-Djenoun and back
distance climbed: 800 metres
time: 12 hours

Made famous by the works of Roger Frison-Roche and preceded by a long and laborious approach which could call for the addition of an intermediary camp (water must be taken with you), the climb to Garet el-Djenoun is one of the most traditional treks on Tefedest and in the whole Sahara.
From Mertoutek follow Oued Dehine to the base of the massif and then climb up along Oued Ti-n-Ekert as far as possible. Start off again at dawn following the Oued for a long stretch. A steep and not

55 top
The spectacular
Garet el-Djenoun
peak dominates
the wadies in the
Tefedest mountains.
Photograph by
B. Brera/K3

difficult ravine of blocks leads to the East Hill and the start of the climb. Approximately 120 metres of sheet rocks and crevices (2nd and 3rd degree) lead to a narrow ledge to be followed to the left. Once around the corner "passage of the moufflon", climb alongside the ravine that cuts the south slope until you come out on the large top clearing. The highest point (2,375 metres) is to the north. On the descent numerous double ropes are required. Those not wishing to climb can stop at the hill. The tour around the mountain is long and spectacular.

55 centre
Approximately 400 metres high, the west face is the most difficult and elegant of Garet el-Djenoun and provides some of the most difficult climbing routes in the Sahara.
Photograph by
Gudrun Bergdhal/
Agence Freestyle

55 bottom
A mountaineer on the elegant grade 2 and 3 sheet rock that precedes the ledge and "passage of the mufflon" on the normal route to Garet el-Djenoun.
Photograph by
Mario Verin

ON THE TASSILI PLATEAU

Discovering the so-called
"Louvre of the Sahara"

The Tassili-n-Ajjer plateau, winter 1933. At the head of a platoon of meharists set out from Fort Gardel (today Djanet), lieutenant Brenans ventured amidst the towers, rocky backdrops and deep canyons that make this range one of the loveliest in the Sahara. Step after step, day after day the column discovered an extraordinary open air museum. Close to Tarmrit, Jabbaren and Sefar hundreds of precipices, caves and natural shelters are decorated with drawings of remarkable beauty, perfectly preserved in the dry desert climate. Since the beginning of the century, explorers in the Libyan, Moroccan and Algerian Sahara had found and described dozens of rock drawing sites. It was however immediately clear that Tassili was something else. Here the drawings seemed to be countless in number and included works of outstanding beauty: oxen, horses, antelopes and huge human figures. Twenty-three years after Brenans, during a sixteen month expedition, the anthropologist Henri Lhoté was at last to complete the inventory of this "Louvre of the Sahara." "The Tassili drawings are an authentic archive and provide a very clear picture of the ancient peoples of the Sahara, of the surges of herdsmen following one after the other, of the foreign influence manifested" as Lhoté wrote two years later in his well-known *To the Discovery Tassili*. He continues "And thanks to them, we can follow the evolution of the fauna and, hence, of the climate and the phases of the gradual drying up that created the desert of today." A great journey through history and art, the trek amidst the Tassili drawings is also a trip through the past of northern Africa. Drawings dating from 8000 years B.C. and thus far more recent than the great European works of cave drawings (date between 30,000 and 12,000 years B.C.), the Tassili drawings embrace a succession of styles, of subjects, of themes.
The first phase (until 4500 B.C.)

known as the "time of the roundheads" contains mainly anthropomorphic figures, flanked at the end by buffaloes and other species such as elephants, hippopotamus and rhinoceros. It is the mark of a hunting people. Next comes the bovid period (4000-1500 B.C.), the expression of animal rearers; their herds of *Bos brachicerus* and *Bos africanus* - are similar to those of upper Egypt in that period. There are pictures of wild animals, scenes of family life

and work in the fields, that bring to mind the modern reality of numerous African ethnic groups such as the Peuls, the Sahel herdsmen. Many of the best works in terms of colour and stylistic elegance belong to this time. Around 1200 B.C. the bovid herdsmen were chased from Tassili by a different ethnic group: a light-skinned people using carts and horses. The drawings of the "horse" period portray a drier landscape, where the hippopotamus and elephant had definitively disappeared. Alongside the magnificent galloping horses appear men armed with spears and shields,

probably dressed in leather armour. Various experts have put forward an attractive suggestion: that these were the Peoples of the Sea of Egyptian tradition, i.e. the Libyans and Cretans allied against Rameses III in 1280 B.C., and the Garamantes mentioned by Herodotus.
The last phase, the "camel" period, dates from the first centuries of the Christian era. The signs of dryness are clear, the most obvious of these being the appearance of the camel. Drawings and characters portray a people not unlike the modern Tuareg. Today, there are more trekkers than scholars on Tassili-n-Ajjer.

56 This large drawing portraying a god is one of the most famous in the Tassili mountains. It dates from the time of the roundheads (up to 4500 B.C.) which was dominated by human figures.
Photograph by Anne Conway

56-57 Marked by a spectacular series of rock towers and canyons, the Tassili-n-Ajjer landscape is one of the most interesting in the Sahara.
Photograph by Mauro Burzio

57 The drawings of Sefar depicting flocks of sheep and herds of goats date from about the year 2000 B.C..
Photograph by Anne Conway

58-59 A few minutes' hike from the Tamrit camp, a picturesque rocky valley features the age-old Tassili cypresses.
Photograph by Anne Conway

Eight hundred kilometres in length and between 50 and 60 wide, this plateau is practically one of the most interesting destinations in the Sahara. It must be covered on foot. Short and not particularly exhausting, the trek across it is one of the most popular in Africa.

The starting point is the town of Djanet, the "pearl of Tassili" surrounded by rocky heights and extensive palm groves. Comprising the four villages of El Mihan, Adjahi, Azzelouaz and Tin Khatama, it offers visitors an airport, a hotel, a market and a Turkish bath ("hamman"), particularly inviting on return from the paths of the plateau. Do not miss the museum devoted to the geology and prehistoric art of Tassili.

Then you walk.

Necessarily accompanied and usually organized over 4 or 5 days, the trek across Tassili is no great adventure in the wilderness but it does offer a series of extraordinary emotions. The deep canyons on the edge of the plateau, the maze of gorges, towers, natural corridors and caves between Tamrit and Sefar form an incredible, fairy tale landscape where the presence of expert Tuareg guides is essential to avoid losing one's bearings. In this true mineral desert the appearance of the huge, millenary cypress trees (the scientific name is *Cupressus dupreziana*, the Tuareg call them *tarout*) in a rocky gorge at the gateway to Tamrit is moving.

The greatest emotion of all is produced by the rock drawings. Even a small tour will include hundreds of them. Among the many, the horse-like antilopes of Tamrit, the bowmen of Tin Tazarift, the family scenes, the great buffalo and the "god of the worshippers" of Sefar and the great characters of Tam Zoumaitek are the most exciting encounters. Back in the valley there is time for a trip to the drawings of Oued Djerat, the rock site of Jabbaren (reached on foot from Sefar in two days) and the splendid dunes of the Erg d'Admer.

USEFUL INFORMATION

Duration: 4 days.
Elevation: from 1,100 to 2,800 metres.
Period: all year round but the middle seasons are best.
The summer is truly scorching and in winter the temperature may fall to -10°C.
Red tape: a visa is required for Algeria. No special permits are required for trekking.
Degree of difficulty: the occasional easy climbing passage (grade I) on the route up to the plateau.
Physical challenge: average-low
Equipment: normal trekking gear
Access routes: Djanet (1,100 metres), the town at the foot of the massif, is linked by daily flights to Algiers. The journey over land is 2,250 kilometres from Algiers and 2,350 from Tunis. From Djanet a wide, easy track, approximately 15 kilometres long, leads to the foot of the plateau (1,300 metres).
Guides and porters on Tassili: it is compulsory to be accompanied by a guide. At Djanet numerous agencies organize treks on the plateau. Baggage is carried by asses or dromedaries.
Detours and peaks: an extra day at Sefar is definitely recommended to admire the drawings of the area without haste. The route on the plateau can be followed eastwards towards Jabbaren, at the centre of another area of great artistic interest. There are no peaks of special interest. The faces of the numerous pinnacles of Tassili offer great opportunities for climbers.
In case of trouble: the short length of the trek and the presence of beasts of burden permit a fairly quick evacuation of any injuried parties.
Maps: there are no detailed maps available.
Guidebooks: general information on the area can be found in *Sahara - guida al deserto* by B. Vaes, G. del Marmol and A. d'Otreppe (Edizioni Futuro, 1987). Also useful are the Guide Bleu *Algérie* (Hachette, 1986) and *Algeria* by Paolo Santacroce (Clup, 1980)
For further reading: the best work for details of the Tassili drawings is *Antiche Civiltà del Sahara* by Massimo Baistrocchi (Mursia, 1986). The exciting story of the exploration of the "Louvre of the Sahara" is to be found in *To the Discovery of Tassili* by Henri Lhoté. Information on its nature and mountaineering history is contained in *Uomini e montagne del Sahara* and in *Tuareg, Tassili, Sahara* both by Mario Fantin (Tamari, 1969). Also of interest is *Lettere dal Sahara* by Alberto Moravia (Bompiani, 1981).

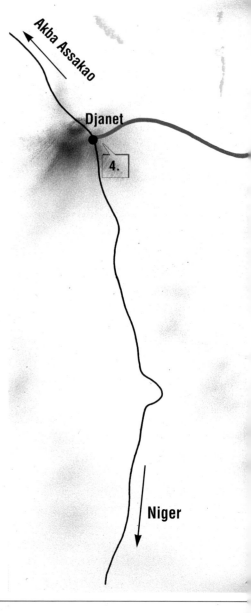

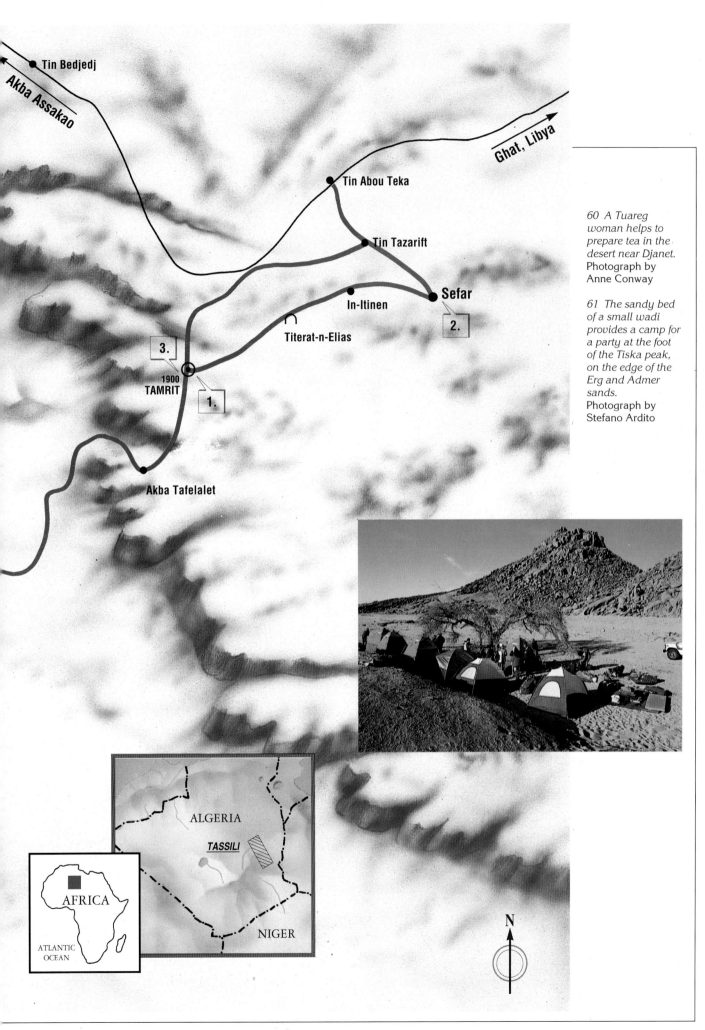

Tin Bedjedj

Akba Assakao

Ghat, Libya

Tin Abou Teka

Tin Tazarift

Sefar

2.

In-Itinen

Titerat-n-Elias

3.

1900
TAMRIT

1.

Akba Tafelalet

60 *A Tuareg
woman helps to
prepare tea in the
desert near Djanet.*
Photograph by
Anne Conway

61 *The sandy bed
of a small wadi
provides a camp for
a party at the foot
of the Tiska peak,
on the edge of the
Erg and Admer
sands.*
Photograph by
Stefano Ardito

AFRICA

ATLANTIC
OCEAN

ALGERIA

TASSILI

NIGER

N

62 top At Terarart, a few kilometres from Djanet, is this splendid bas-relief depicting oxen at water.
Photograph by Anne Conway

FIRST DAY
from Djanet to Tamrit
distance climbed: 700 metres
distance descended: 50 metres
time: 4 hours 30 minutes

The first day of the trek is mainly of scenic interest. After a boring and sunny start the path comes to a sandy hollow with a beautiful natural arch, then enters the deep, spectacular canyon of Akba Tafelalet; you leave this to the left (north) with a series of easy climbing passages. When you reach the edge of the plateau the landscape changes: continue across the barren and striking plateau to the permanent camp of Tamrit (1,900 metres). Not to be missed are the millenary cypress wood and frescoes of hunters.

62 centre
An undemanding, flat path crosses the stony plateau between the Tamrit camp and the edge of the deep Akba Tafelalet canyon.
Photograph by Stefano Ardito

62 bottom A few minutes' hike from Tamrit the path for Tin Abou Teka and Tan Zoumaitek skirts a magnificent natural arch.
Photograph by Marco Majrani

62-63 The area surrounding Djanet is full of bizarre

spectacular rock formations shaped by wind erosion.
Photograph by Anne Conway

63 bottom left
The springs not far from the Tassili cypresses have provided water for goats, donkeys and camels for thousands of years.
Photograph by Anne Conway

63 bottom right
A party of trekkers crosses the rocky valley with the Tassili cypresses.
Photograph by Stefano Ardito

SECOND DAY
from Tamrit to Sefar
distance climbed: 200 metres
distance descended: 150 metres
time: 4 hours

Not long and, above all, on the flat, this stage leads to the heart of Tassili. Start by plunging amid the pinnacles and rocky scenery and advancing to the caves of Titerat-n-Elias, in the past the home of one of the most ancient

settlements on the plateau; proceed towards In-Itinen and its bovid drawings. Then you go to Sefar and camp in a spectacular maze of rocky gorges abounding with prehistoric sites. Excursions around Sefar will take up the afternoon of the day of arrival and the next morning. Those wishing to learn more about Sefar should schedule an extra day in the area. Not to be missed, in any case, are the frescoes of the "god of the worshippers" and the "small moufflons".

64 left Near Sefar the Tassili plateau is marked by a spectacular series of sandstone aiguilles and ravines.
Photograph by Stefano Ardito

64 top right Sunset on the heights that close the Sefar valley; the eyes scan one of the most beautiful views in the Tassili mountains and indeed all the mountains of the Sahara.
Photograph by Stefano Ardito

64 centre right A Tuareg guide explains the history and secrets of a painted cave close to Sefar to a party of trekkers.
Photograph by Anne Conway

64 bottom right Just a few minutes walk from Sefar, this spectacular picture of a buffalo is one of the most famous of Tassili.
Photograph by Anne Conway

THIRD DAY

from Sefar to Tamrit
distance climbed: 250 metres
distance descended: 300 metres
time: 4 hours 30 minutes

The return to Tamrit is via a different and more spectacular route, passing the remarkable rocky massif of Tin Tazarift, also richly frescoed, the rocks of Tin Abou Teka (1,600 metres) overlooking a very deep canyon and the enormous Tan Zoumaitek drawing, completed over six different epochs.
Tamrit is reached by passing through the magnificent canyon with cypresses, some having a diameter of two metres.

FOURTH DAY

from Tamrit to Djanet
distance climbed: 100 metres
distance descended: 500 metres
time: 3 hours 30 minutes

For the return to the valley you take a different route from that of the ascent; it is that used by the beasts of burden on the outward journey. The path leads to the edge of the plateau, slightly farther north than the other, and descends into another lovely, striking canyon before returning in the end to the large hollow of the first stage. Beside the natural arch you will encounter the path followed on the outward journey that leads back to the trail.

65 top Between Tamrit and Sefar the Tassili trail passes through numerous sandy hollows surrounded by rock faces fashioned by wind erosion.
Photograph by Anne Conway

65 centre top A trekker pauses before crossing the most characteristic rocky arch of Tin Tazarift.
Photograph by Stefano Ardito

65 centre bottom On all treks on the Tassili plateau baggage is entrusted to donkeys as the rocky terrain of these mountains is too awkward for camels.
Photograph by Anne Conway

65 bottom A party of trekkers follows the steep stony path from Tamrit down to the Akba Tafelalet canyon.
Photograph by

65 right The aiguilles and natural arches of the characteristic rocky massif of Tin Tazarift, crossed on the return from Sefar to Tamrit, will amaze the trekker.
Photograph by Stefano Ardito

IN THE DOGON FALAISE

An encounter with one of the most fascinating peoples in Africa

In the middle of the barren Sahel landscape, the majestic rocky Bandiagara cliff dominates everyday life and the huts and villages of one of the most extraordinary peoples in Africa. Three distinct ethnic groups, the Humeré on the plain, the Gondo to the east and the Tombo at Bandiagara and nearby, the Dogon - today just under 300,000 in number - were chased from the plain crossed by the winding Niger at an uncertain time in our Middle Ages.
Only superficially islamicized, they conserve a highly complex animistic faith particularly rich in symbolic meanings.
All their villages are built around a central Togu Na, the "house of the men", decorated with elegant and characteristic panels of inlaid wood. All the houses have unusual conic barns and splendid carved locks.
The centre of the Dogon universe is the wall of "ground standing up". Three hundred metres high and two hundred kilometres long, the falaise of Bandiagara cuts across the plain diagonally, seemingly protecting the villages that nest at its foot.
High up, far above the houses and the barns of Tireli, Teli, Banani, and other villages, the great rocky wall is home to the constructions of the Tellem, the mysterious people who preceded the Dogon in this area and were probably chased by them. The terraces and caves appearing in the mighty wall have been used as burial places for centuries, first by one and then by the other people and the whole area is prohibited to outsiders.
Bird hunters, gatherers of eggs and guano and the petit responsible for burying the dead climb the wall with the aid of baobab bark ropes and wooden pegs fixed in holes and fissures in the rock. It is a spectacle that makes even the most expert mountaineer shudder.
It was the French anthropologist Marcel Griaule, in 1931, who explored and told the rest of the world of the elaborate Dogon traditions and their complex cosmogony. After reaching the falaise during a two year long expedition between Dakar and Djibouti, the anthropologist remained for thirty-three days conversing with Ogotemmeli, a blind hunter from the village of Ogol, who disclosed to him the secrets of the Dogon world and culture: the result of this encounter between two worlds is God of Water one of the most famous anthropology books of all times. Among the most interesting aspects of the Dogon civilization are their conception of the universe (distributed over 14 solar systems), the highly elaborate wooden masks used in dances and celebrations, the village architecture and their funeral rites. And, of course, the great festivities: the *Sigui* held every

66 Seen from the top of the Dogon Falaise the villages below appear even more charming.

67 Narrow ledges and shaky wooden ladders lead up the Dogon Falaise. Access to these rocks is normally taboo for outsiders and is only possible if expressly authorized by the village elders.
Photographs by Mario Verin

sixty years, the *Agguet* in honour of their ancestors, the *Ondonfile* that precedes the first rains and the *Fête des masques* lasting five days and celebrated between April and May in all the villages.

It is impossible on a trip to Mali not to dedicate a few days to the Dogon and their extraordinary world. The few days - usually one or two - devoted by most tours to the villages around the falaise are by no means sufficient for a true appreciation of the remarkable cultural wealth of this people. Here hiking is by far the best solution. At the slow pace of trekking, you can come into contact with the people, observe the architecture and landscapes without haste, reach the villages least touched by tourism. In other parts of Africa hiking is a sport but this is a walk dedicated to tradition, culture, people.

The fascination of Mali does not end with the encounter with the Dogon. On the boundary between black Africa and Islam, where the desert gives way to the steppe, this huge country (1,240,000 square kilometres and a population of eight million) saw, between the eighth and sixteenth centuries, the flourishing empires of Ghana, Mali and Sonrai. Well established along the bend in the Niger, their black governors converted to Islam controlled the great caravan routes across the Sahara. In 1324 the emperor Kankan Moussa went on a pilgrimage to Mecca taking with him a following of sixty thousand people and 150 kilos of gold.

In the nineteenth century Mali co-existed in the dreams and plans of the European adventurers - two thousand kilometres north-west - with the sources of the Nile and the great lakes of eastern Africa.

The first to arrive, in 1796, on the banks of the Niger, the great waterway of western Africa, was the Scottish doctor Mungo Park. His *Journey to the Heart of Africa* is one of the first (and still one of the most exciting) works on the continent of mysteries.

Then Timbuktu, the mysterious city on the edge of the Sahara, became the coveted destination for adventurers of all Europe.

It was again Mungo Park who came close to it in 1805, then the Scottish

captain Gordon Laing reached it only to be killed by the Tuareg. The Frenchman René Caillié, at 27 years of age, was the first to describe the city to the Europeans. He reached it in 1828 from the coast of Guinea and, eluding the suspicion of the Tuareg by disguising himself as an Arab, stayed for two weeks, describing it as a "heap of clay houses surrounded by immense plains of extremely barren moving sand." Today the principal cities of the country conserve clear traces of its ancient splendour. Djenné has walls in unbaked clay, finely decorated palaces, the great Mosque studded with crenellating and towers.

Other elegant mosques can be seen at San, Mopti and, of course, Timbuktu. Bearing witness to the skill of the local architects in the use of unbaked clay are the saho, the elegant "houses of the young" found in the Bozo fishing villages on the banks of the Niger.

River navigation on pirogues with large sails is one of the most interesting experiences of the journey. In the small and large markets on the river banks, fishermen and river boatmen trade with the Bambara peasants and the Peul herdsmen of the brousse, the barren plain stretching from the banks as far as the eye can see.

In the north-east of the country the trails leading from Timbuktu and

Gao towards the border with Algeria and the Niger are still controlled by the warrior Tuareg tribes. Elsewhere Africa shows the visitor deserts, savannahs, animals and great mountains; western Africa is the place of peoples, cultures, traditions. A world in which Mali - and the magnificent trek through the architecture, rocks and traditions of the Dogon - deserves a place of honour.

68 Masked cerimonies play an important role in the Dogon culture in Mali. The photograph shows a group of dancers from Bandiagara wearing antelope masks. Photograph by Stefano Ardito

69 left A Dogon girl participates in the dance wearing a costume of shells, beads and baobab fruit. Photograph by Stefano Ardito

69 right A scene from the Fête des Masques in Tireli, at the foot of the Dogon Falaise. This celebration lasts five days and is held between April and May in all the local villages. Photograph by Mario Verin

USEFUL INFORMATION

70 Studded with crenellation and towers, the Great Mosque is the most interesting monument in the ancient caravan town of Djenné.
Photograph by Marco Majrani

71 left Near Bandiagara the village women leave onions, chopped and mixed with herbs, to dry.
Photograph by Mario Verin

71 right A trekker on the ledge dominating the Dogon Falaise as the long shadows of sunset embrace these extraordinary rock formations.
Photograph by Mario Verin

Duration: 6 days.
Elevation: from 300 to 800 metres.
Period: Hiking is possible in Mali all year round. From December to February the climate is mild but the harmattan, the desert wind, makes the landscape a little dull. From March to May it is very hot. The rainy season (June-September) creates a few problems on the trail but brings more attractive light.
Red tape: A visa is required to enter Mali; no special permits are needed for the trek.
Degree of difficulty: none.
Physical challenge: average-low.
Equipment: normal trekking gear. Camping is possible in the villages and accommodation is cheap in the maisons de passage found in all the Dogon villages. In this case a sleeping bag and mattress are needed but no tent.
Access routes: from Bamako, the capital of Mali, a good asphalt road

Guides and porters: a guide can be hired at Bandiagara or Sangha.
Detours and peaks: there are no "peaks" in the area except for the pinnacles and towers much exploited in recent years by European climbers. There are many possible variations towards other villages at the foot of the falaise which, beyond Kani-Kombodè, goes south-west for another thirty kilometres or so. More so than in any other area described in this book, the trek among the Dogon can be modified as desired according to the weather and time available and the interests of the trekkers.
In case of trouble: the trails running not far from the foot of the cliff and leading to most of the villages make it fairly easy and quick to return to Sangha or Bandiagara.
Maps: there are no detailed maps of the area.
Guidebooks: information on Mali is found in *Niger, Mali, Mauritania,*

N

leads in 610 kilometres to Mopti, the main port on the Niger. This can be reached by plane or using the riverboat services that run during the rainy season. From Mopti a trouble-free trail leads in 65 kilometres to Bandiagara and in another 44 kilometres to Sangha. As well as private vehicles, the route can be followed using buses or the bush taxi, picturesque overcrowded cars or vans. Between the main Dogon villages transfers can be made on the back of a small motocycle *(mobylette).*

Burkina Faso by Alex Newton (Lonely Planet, 1992), the Guide Bleu *Au Mali et au Niger* (Hachette, 1980) or *Sahara - Guida al Deserto* published by Edizioni Futuro (1983).
For further reading: the most famous book on the Dogon is *God of Water* by Marcel Griaule (Bompiani, 1968). Also of interest is *Les Dogons du Mali* by Gérard Beaudoin (Armand Colin, 1984), *Journey to the Heart of Africa* by Mungo Park (Casa Usher, 1990) and *Journey to Timbuktu* by René Caillé (Cierre, 1993).

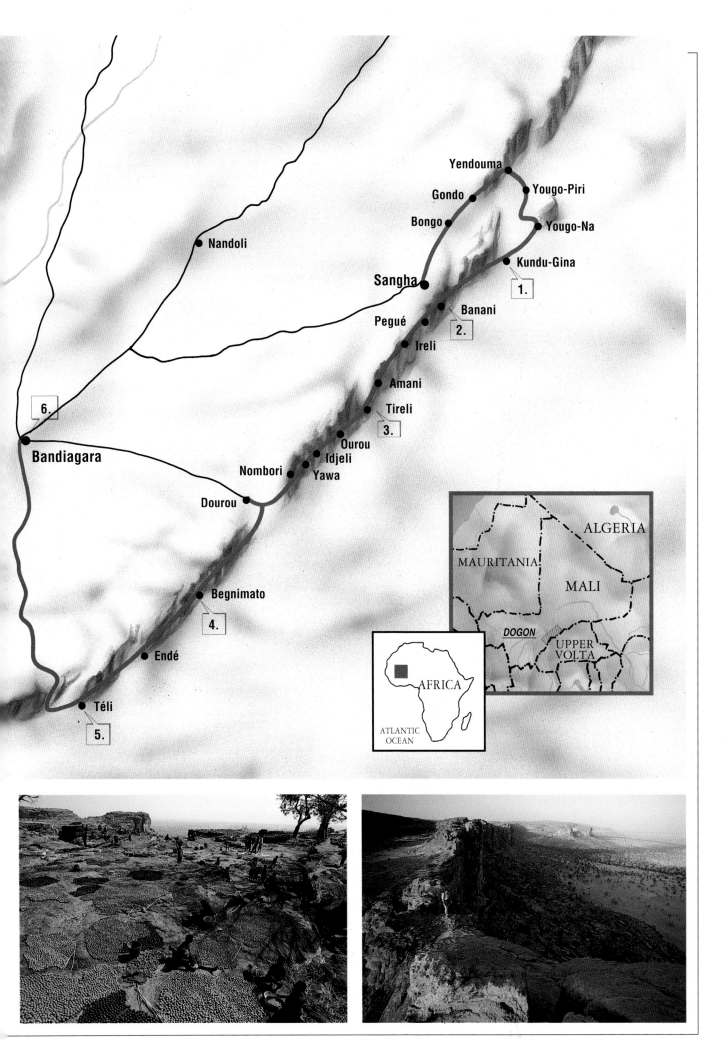

Yendouma

Yougo-Piri

Gondo

Bongo

Yougo-Na

Kundu-Gina

1.

Nandoli

Sangha

Banani

2.

Pegué

Ireli

Amani

Tireli

3.

Ourou

Idjeli

6.

Nombori

Yawa

Bandiagara

Dourou

Begnimato

4.

Endé

Téli

5.

ALGERIA

MAURITANIA

MALI

DOGON

UPPER
VOLTA

AFRICA

ATLANTIC
OCEAN

FIRST DAY

from Sangha to Kundu-Gina
distance climbed: 150 metres
distance descended: 450 metres
time: 6 hours 30 minutes

The dusty village of Sangha, full of huge baobab trees and overlooking the falaise from above, is for nearly all travellers their first contact with the vertical world of the Dogon. After a stop in the village - an interesting and colourful market is held every 5 days - walk northwards down the dirt track to Bongo which then descends to the Gondo plain at the foot of the cliff. Proceed at the foot of the rocks to Yendouma and continue on the plain to the rise between the baobab trees leading to the plateau and the village of Yougo-Piri. A rapid descent leads to Yougo-Na from where you proceed on the level through fields of millet, onions and sarghum to Kundu-Gina.

72 top The picture shows a row of fields given over to onion growing.
Photograph by Marco Majrani

72 centre
A view from the top of the Falaise looking down on the village of Yendouma.
Photograph by Cl. Jaccoux/ Agence Freestyle

72 bottom
Clearly visible are the details of the
original constructions of the Dogon Falaise inhabitants as seen here in the village of Yendouma.
Photograph by Cl. Jaccoux/ Agence Freestyle

72-73 Some of the houses in the village of Sangha set amid lush green fields; many of the crops here are grown in water.
Photograph by Cl. Jaccoux/ Agence Freestyke

73 bottom left Careful observation of the Dogon houses reveals truly remarkable craftmanship, such as these wooden shutters finely inlaid with anthropomorphic motifs.
Photograph by Cl. Jaccoux/ Agence Freestyle

73 bottom right The woman in the picture is busy storing millet in the granary; note the inlaid shutter and the relief designs on the walls of the building.
Photograph by Mario Verin

SECOND DAY
from Kundu-Gina to Banani
distance climbed: 100 metres
distance descended: 100 metres
time: 5 hours

An interesting day at the foot of the highest section of the cliff here rising to 300 metres and more. The route follows that of the previous day as far as the large village of Banani; here various lovely Togu Na deserve a visit, as well as the characteristic spring that gushes out right at the foot of the rocks. Lovers of comfort can even climb on foot up the steep path that uses a long flight of steps in a deep crack in the falaise and spend another night in the not excessive comfort of the hotels of Sangha.

74 top
A characteristic anthropomorphic house in the village of Banani.
Photograph by Mario Verin

74 bottom
The houses of many Dogon villages, in the picture those of Izelli, are often up against the Bandiagara Falaise.
Photograph by Cl. Jaccoux/ Agence Freestyle

THIRD DAY
from Banani to Tireli
distance climbed: 100 metres
distance descended: 130 metres
time: 5 hours

A far from long and tiring stage offering the trekker an encounter with some of the most charming Dogon villages. It passes through Pegué, Tireli and Amani: near the latter is the interesting, small lake of Koo with its crocodiles.

To admire the great rock face from afar, you can go away from it and camp for the night in the magnificent red sand dunes.

FOURTH DAY
from Tireli to Begnimato
distance climbed: 100 metres
distance descended: 80 metres
time: 6 hours

A rather long stage (it can be broken by spending the night at Nombori) leading to the falaise area less patronized by trekkers and tourists with vehicles. Continue to walk through fields and solitary trees, passing Ourou, Idjeli, Nombori and Yawa along the way. At the last village another spectacular path climbs in a rocky gorge and in an hour's hike (1 hour 30 minutes longer return) leads to the edge of the plateau and Dourou, a large village 18 kilometres and 4-5 hours' hike from Bandiagara.

FIFTH DAY
from Begnimato to Téli
distance climbed: 300 metres
distance descended: 50 metres
time: 5 hours

Now outside the best known and most popular part of the falaise, proceed at the foot of the rocks, here decidedly lower and less spectacular, in the direction of Yabatalu, Endé and Téli, a picturesque village near which are some quite interesting waterfalls and rock drawings.

SIXTH DAY
from Dourou to Djiguibombo to Bandiagara
distance climbed: 350 metres
time: 1 hour 30 minutes - 6 hours

The trek ends with the short but steep path climbing between the rocks to the village of Djiguibombo, linked to Bandiagara by a reasonable trail 20 kilometres long. Those who do not find a lift or wanting to finish the trek without "cheating" will take another 4 or 5 hours on foot.

74-75
The photograph shows the incredible development of the Falaise in Mali and the unmistakable and characteristic village of Izelli.
Photograph by
Cl. Jaccoux/
Agence Freestyle

75 top
The photograph shows how close the Dogon buildings whether homes, stores or other, are built to the rock formation.
Photograph by
Cl. Jaccoux/
Agence Freestyle

THE PEAKS AND PLATEAUX OF THE SEMIEN

On the highest and most spectacular mountains in Ethiopia

Rolling plateaux and impressive walls of vertical rock, villages seemingly unchanged since the dawn of time, forests of heather and towering lobelias, graceful endemic animals such as the *Gelada* baboons and the local ibex. Ethiopia is a country of surprises and contrasts and the Semien, the majestic mountain chain that cuts across the north of the country, is certainly where the contrasts and surprises are most obvious. For those arriving from the north along the ancient route from Axum and Asmara, the massif appears a single rocky wall twenty kilometres or more wide, flanked to the north east by the phantasmagoric pinnacles of the Tsellemtì massif. From here, nothing betrays the rolling, gentle plateau that stretches above this vertical universe. Most visitors arrive from the south, however, from the historic city of Gondar, easily reached by plane from the capital Addis Abeba. In this case, you should first visit the church of Debra Berham Selassie with its magnificent 1682 frescoes and the extraordinary castle built between 1637 and 1680 by the Emperor Fasilides and his son Yohannes I the "Right one". Then follow the winding road built by Italian engineers in 1937-1939 to the large village of Debarek, on Saturdays the venue for a picturesque market. From here proceed towards the mountains. It takes a day and a half of zigzagging through cultivated fields and valleys, woods of tree-like heather and juniper and stony ground to discover the cliffs, pinnacles and most spectacular side of the Semien. As everywhere in Ethiopia, it is the people that amaze most. As at the foot of the great mountains of Nepal - and unlike all the most popular treks in Africa - on the Semien you walk from village to village, along the mule tracks and paths used for many centuries by wayfarers of all

76 From the Gich refuge (3,600 metres) the eyes sweep over the gentle reliefs of the plateau coloured by the sunset.

77 The plain suddenly appears from the ridge connecting Imet Gogo (3,936 metres) to Gidir Got. In the foreground is a group of lobelia.
Photographs by Stefano Ardito

kinds. Old men with the appearance and beards of patriarchs, Coptic priests and deacons, very clearly venerated, women elegantly dressed despite the extreme poverty, caravans of donkeys heading for the markets of Aberghina, Debarek or even Gondar and young herdsmen dressed in goat skins and rags. Along the path, women suddenly appear from nowhere to sell *talla*, a bitter home-made beer, to passers-by. Constantly along the way you will encounter caravans on the move or porters carrying timber or other goods. Everywhere, even in the wildest parts of the massif you unexpectedly come across huts with cultivated fields, pens for the animals, wells, a network of paths: a human presence that seems hidden in the

folds of the plateau. There is also nature. Culminating in the 4,620 metres of Ras Dashan (or Ras Dejen) and the 4,430 metres of Bwahit and flanked by countless smaller peaks above four thousand metres, the highest range in Ethiopia is still - despite the intrusive presence of man who has cleared woods and hunted almost everywhere - an extraordinary open-air museum of flora, fauna and geology. Made of schists, sandstone and granite, the massif is covered with remarkable vegetation, similar but different from that of the other great peaks of Africa. Spiky acacias accompany the journey from Axum or Gondar towards the mountains, followed by cultivated fields.

Then, up to 3,500-3,800 metres are the forests of heather, hypericum, hygenia and juniper. Unlike those of Mount Kenya, Kilimanjaro and Ruwenzori - fascinating but extremely dense and often oppressive - these Ethiopian woods have a less menacing and more pleasant appearance, reminiscent of the ilex groves and cork plantations of the mountains overlooking the Mediterranean.

Towards 3,500 metres (and up to 4,000) helichrysum and lobelia appear, although of different species from those present on the ranges farther south.

These plants will accompany you through the meadows to the edge of the great cliffs plunging northwards. Here, amid the pastures and the last fields, you will meet packs of bawling Gelada baboons *(Theropitecus galad)*, graceful monkeys with a characteristic long coat, and less often the Semien ibex *(Capra ibex walia)* one of the rarest species in Africa.

Usually, the latter are seen from the edges of the cliffs, as they run surefootedly along the narrow ledges and the steepest of grassy slopes that break up the great walls. Completing the list of local species in the Park is the Semien fox *(Simenya simensis)* plus leopards, colobus, serval, duiker and the odd hyrax. Hyenas appear quite frequently around the fields and villages.

Without technical problems, always extremely fascinating, the trek through the valleys and peaks of the Semien can be organized in two ways. The first, described here, is basically a visit to the Park.

A route taking 6-7 days (or less if you go to the mountains by car) and bringing you into contact with the loveliest and easiest peaks of Imet Gogo (3,936 metres), Inatye (4,070 metres) and Bwahit (4,430 metres).

It is longer and more tiring if you include Ras Dashan (4,620 metres), the highest peak in Ethiopia. In this case you must descend from the 4,100 metres of the ridge between Chennek and Bwahit to the 2,900 metres of the deep Ainsyo river valley and then climb again to the village of Ambikwo and the peak. You are highly recommended to proceed down towards Addi Arcai instead of climbing up again towards Chennek. The whole route takes nearly two weeks.

Relatively popular until the 1974 revolution, the Semien suffered greatly during the clashes - which continued until 1992 - between Mengistu's soldiers and the TPLF, Tigrai Liberation Front, later to become the country's interim government. At the time of writing Ethiopia is at last peaceful again and has quickly reopened to tourism. The parks and monasteries, religious holidays and waterfalls, lakes and peoples deserve this renewed interest.

In the Semien, however, the lodges set afire or bombed, as well as the drastic reduction in the numbers of ibex because of hunting by the soldiers on both sides, are clear signs of the war.

Not until the autumn of 1994 did the construction of a new refuge hut at Gich show that times have finally changed.

At the time of writing the Semien offers the possibility of hiking far from the hordes of north American and European tourists that crowd the paths of Kilmanjaro and Mount Kenya.

This fascination is counterbalanced, of course, by the poor knowledge on the part of the local guides and the Addis Abeba agencies of the interests and needs of trekkers arriving from afar.

A little attention to supplies and to the route proposed is the best guarantee of an inspiring and untroubled adventure.

78-79 An obligatory point of passage for every visit made to the Semien massif Is the historical town of Gondar which will amaze the visitor with *its castle built between 1637 and 1680 at the order of the Emperors Fasilidas and Yohannes I.* Photograph by Stefano Ardito

USEFUL INFORMATION

Duration: 7 days.
Elevation: from 3,020 to 4,430 metres.
Period: from October to May. In March and April there may be the odd day of rain coming from the Indian Ocean.
Red tape: no visa is needed for Ethiopia. Entrance fees to the Semien National Park are paid at Debarek.
Degree of difficulty: no technical problems but the stage between Gich and Chennek includes some aerial and exposed stretches.
Physical challenge: average. Some stages are rather tedious and tiring because of the length, altitude and exposure to the sun.

Equipment: normal trekking gear, a tent is required.
Access routes: Debarek (3,020 metres) is 100 kilometres on a good road from Gondar. The journey takes approximartely 3 hours by car, 4-5 by bus. At the beginning of the village is the Semien National Park office where you pay the small entrance fee to the protected area and the charges for the rangers that can accompany parties.
Guides and porters: at Debarek you can hire guides, porters, beasts of burden (usually mules) and their drivers. You are also advised to go accompanied by a Park ranger (see above): this is a considerable help for spotting fauna.
Detours and peaks: along the route are the peaks of Imet Gogo (3,936 metres), Inatye (4,070 metres) and

Bwahit (4,430 metres).
A popular variation goes in two days from Chennek to Ras Dashan (or Ras Dejen, 4,620 metres), the highest peak in Ethiopia and the fourth highest in Africa. In this case the descent along the Ainsyo river valley to Addi Arcai is recommended.
In case of trouble: the dirt track crossing the Park to Chennek can be used for the evacuation of any injured person. But vehicles are very rare!
Maps: excellent but hard to find is the Swiss map 1:100,000 *Semien National Park.* Of interest but scarce in detail are the maps 1:400,000 *Gondar and Macallé* published by the Italian IGM.
Guidebooks: summary information on the massif is contained in the

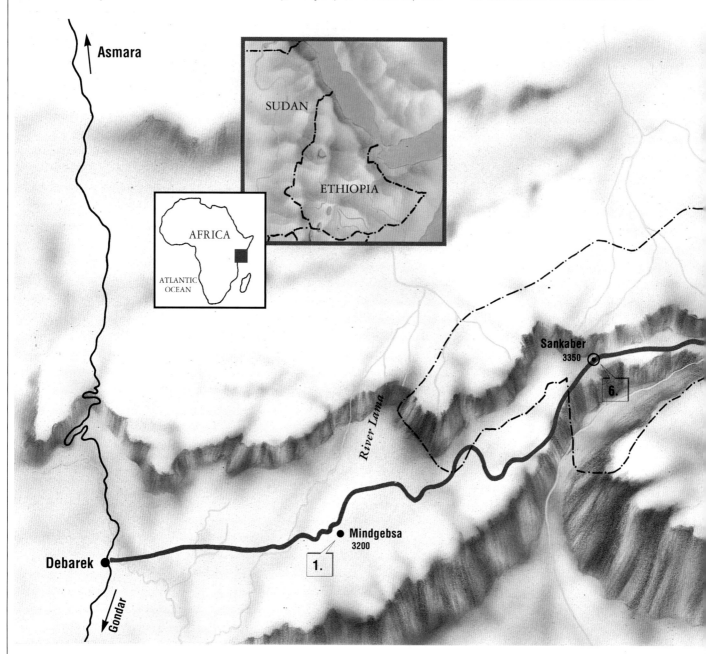

brochure *Semien - the Roof of Africa* (Ethiopian Tourist Trading Corporation, 1986).

Tourist information on Ethiopia is to be found in the Italian Touring Club guide *Africa Orientale Italiana* (1938). Some details on the Semien are found in the first edition of *Backpacker's Africa* by H. Bradt (Bradt Publications, 1983).

For further reading: of interest in English are *The Blue Nile* by Alan Moorehead (1962, the present edition is by Penguin) which contains the story of European exploration of the plateau and the enthralling *The Sign and the Seal* by Graham Hancock (Mandarin, 1992) on the Arch of Alliance which is central to the Ethiopian Christian church.

81 left Aerial and spectacular, the Imet Gogo peak (3,936 metres) is one of the most scenic in Semien; it is a couple of hours from the Gich hut.

81 right Even in the poorest huts the preparation of coffee follows a long and compicated rite. This is the village of Argin, not far from the Chennek camp. Photographs by Stefano Ardito

82 top The castle of Gondar was built in the same style as the Portuguese fortresses constructed in the 16th century on the coasts of Africa.

82 centre The old track between Debarek and the first rises of the Semien chain.

82 bottom Two peasants and their mule travel to the weekly market on the mule track between Mindgebsa and Debarek.

82-83 On the second day of the trek a short detour from the trail to Sankaber provides the opportunity to see north of the plateau, where the park begins.

FIRST DAY
from Debarek to Mindgebsa
distance climbed: 470 metres
distance descended: 300 metres
time: 3 hours 30 minutes

After leaving Debarek, the trail towards the Semien zigzags into a series of deep gorges. Many groups of trekkers start off with the long stage (7 hours) towards Sankaber.

It is far better to start with this short, trouble-free half-stage which can be covered in an afternoon, after spending the morning on preparations or even the transfer from Gondar to Debarek.

After approximately one kilometre on a dirt track descend to cross the Lama river, climb up to a pass and descend again into a second ravine. A rather tiring climb leads to the scattered village of Mindgebsa (3,200 metres approximately). You can camp in several places here, in particular near a school or at the end of the village, past a cool and copious spring.

SECOND DAY
from Mindgebsa to Gich
distance climbed: 850 metres
distance descended: 450 metres
time: 7 hours

A long but interesting day introducing you to the Semien environment with its heather "tree" woods, lovely lobelia and the packs of *Gelada* baboons that can often be sighted at Sankaber and in the Jinbar Wenz valley. After leaving Mindgebsa behind, descend in the beautiful valley of Amgora Wenz and for the first time you will see the north face of the plateau between the Tirf and Aman Amba peaks where you enter the Park. A lovely grassy plain, then a section of the road crossways, monotonous and sunny, lead to the wood and the ruins of the Sankaber lodge (3,350 metres). Descend into another valley then climb up again on the road - wonderful view of the Gidir Got cliffs - and then you take the path to Gich. After fording the Jinbar Wenz, climb to the village (3,500 metres) and then to the Gich camp (3,600 metres) surrounded by splendid lobelia.

83 bottom left A party on the good path in the Jinbar Wenz valley. They are not far from the steep climb that leads to the village and camp of Gich.

83 bottom right Rudimentary but cosy, the Gich refuge hut is the only one remaining on the Semien after the devastation wrought by the civil war that brought bloodshed to Ethiopia until 1992. Photographs by Stefano Ardito

THIRD DAY

from Gich to Imet Gogo and back
distance climbed: 400-500 metres
time: 3-4 hours

From Gich it is certainly worth devoting a day to the nearby and spectacular edge of the plateau, from where you can admire numerous rocky pinnacles and the distant Tsellemtì massif. A good path through the meadows zigzags westwards and in about an hour leads to the edge of the walls.
To the left a section crossways and then an aerial and easy rocky ridge lead to the Imet Gogo peak (3,936 metres), one of the best scenic spots on the mountain. Set off again north-eastwards on the edge of the plateau, followed in zigzags for a certain while before returning to the route and the climb to Gich. This stage can be prolonged westwards in the direction of Gidir Got.

FOURTH DAY

from Gich to Inatye and Chennek
distance climbed: 780 metres
distance descended: 680 metres
time: 6 hours 30 minutes

A magnificent day offering the most spectacular views of the entire trek, on the edge of the majestic walls that defend the Semien plateau from the east. Start with a pleasant descent to the Jinbar Wenz, across a beautiful forest of heather and lobelias. After fording the river, climb through the fields of barley and then the meadows to the dirt track. Follow this for a few hundred metres then go left on the gentle slopes to the rocks that form the Inatye summit (4,070 metres). Continue to the right (south-east) to the edge of the rock faults and start to descend on the easy grassy slopes towards the deep Belegez Wenz valley, where you find Argin and the Chennek camp. A descent on very steep, grassy slopes with a number of spectacular views above the walls leads to the valley bottom. In a few minutes you will be up at the Chennek camp (3,700 metres), the most spectacular of the Semien.

84 top From the top of Imet Gogo the view sweeps over numerous rock towers. The awkward grassy ledges crossing the rock faces are the favourite habitat of the Semien ibex.

84 centre The ridge to the west of Imet Gogo gives a panoramic view of the rock pinnacles of Tsellemti. These dominate the deep Ainsyo river valley and the path to Addi Arcai.

84 bottom The camp and the Chennek heights offer the trekker an extraordinary view of the great rock faces that close the Semien to the east. To the fore are the tree-like heathers characteristic of the massif.

FIFTH DAY
from Chennek to Bwahit and back
distance climbed: 700 metres
time: 4 hours

A short day but one of great interest on which you will reach the Bwahit peak, the highest in the Park and at last overlook the Ras Dashan massif; you will quite possibly see large packs of *Gelada* baboons and far away on the ledges the graceful Semien ibex. Start to climb up a long, broad path that after just over half an hour should be abandoned to keep, farther left, on the edge of the rock faults where monkeys and ibex are often sighted. After leaving the path that descends to the very deep valley of the river Ainsyo to the left continue through rocks and lobelias, skirting some of the steeper climbs to the Bwahit peak (4,430 metres). On the way down, you will descend quickly on the northern slope of the mountain back to the path leading to the camp.

85 top The Bwahit peak (4,430 metres) provides a backdrop to the Chennek camp.

85 centre A sprinkling of snow whitens the rocks and gravel on Bwahit, at 4,430 metres the highest mountain in the park.

85 bottom The last light of day illuminates the isolated countryside of the Semien plateau near the village of Abergina.
Photographs by Stefano Ardito

SIXTH DAY
from Chennek to Sankaber
distance climbed: 550 metres
distance descended: 900 metres
time: 5-6 hours

The return to Debarek starts with a long but interesting day of zigzags; this should be preceded by a visit to the Argin village reached (one hour extra return) from the beginning of the dirt track. Follow this, climbing at length across the mountain until you come out on the plateau; cross it leaving the village of Abergina to the left. Slightly farther on you will pick up the outward route which is followed to Sankaber.

SEVENTH DAY
from Sankaber to Debarek
distance climbed: 250 metres
distance descended: 600 metres
time: 5 hours 30 minutes

The last day of the trek retraces the outward journey. After the first stretch crossways and the meadow highlands, leave the Park through the heather woods of the Angora Wenz valley. Back at Mindegbsa you tackle the last zigzags that lead to Debarek.

RUWENZORI:
THE MOUNTAINS OF THE MOON

The two routes to the wildest
mountain in Africa

86-87 The path climbing from Mutsora to the Kalongi Hut passes through a splendid tropical forest.
Photograph by Marco Majrani

"One of my men attracted my gaze towards the mountain shouting: a mountain rising! I saw a particularly unusually-shaped cloud, of the best silver colour, with the appearance and proportions of a peak crowned with snow... Then I realized that it was not a cloud but a very solid and real mass, a genuine mountain covered with snow."

It was 24 May 1888 and Henry Morton Stanley, one of the most famous names in African exploration, was camped near Nsabè, on Lake Albert, at the springs of the White Nile. Seventeen years had passed since Stanley's encounter with Livingstone at Ujiji - "Doctor Livingstone I presume?" - and this was the Anglo-American journalist and adventurer's third expedition to black Africa. This time he was heading for the Equator to save Emin Pasha and his besieged garrison. But the sharp eye of that unknown porter added a merit to the expedition: the discovery of the mysterious Ruwenzori.

Thanks to Stanley, the legend of the "Mountains of the Moon", the source of the Nile, mentioned by Ptolemy and numerous Arab writers, became a reality. Impressive and wild, Ruwenzori is a truly magnificent mountain. The height - 5,119 metres the highest peak flanked by twenty or so satellites and minor peaks - makes it the third highest mountain in Africa after Kilimanjaro and Kenya and before Ras Dashan and the other great peaks of Ethiopia.

It is immediately clear to the Europeans that this is a special mountain. A high peak, mysterious, a little shady, constantly hidden by the clouds that here, on the border between the immense basins of the Congo and Nile, are particularly persistent. The chain has a complex topography, divided into six mountains - Stanley, Emin, Gessi, Speke, Baker and Luigi di Savoia - numbering a good 24 peaks over 4,000 metres. Today on the border

between Zaire and Uganda, a hundred years ago Ruwenzori marked the boundary between the colonial ambitions of Great Britain and those of King Leopold of Belgium. These were the years of the Scramble for Africa, the race by the European powers to secure for themselves the wealth of an entire continent. Directly on the heels of the explorers came the missionaries, road builders and political representatives of the colonial powers. With them were scientists and mountaineers.

The first to attempt the ascent of Ruwenzori, in 1891, was the German naturalist Franz Stuhlmann, who climbed from the Congo side (today Zaire). A way was opened in the impenetrable forests above Mutwanga until they came out on the ridges at 4,200 metres where today the Kyondo refuge hut stands in a very sorry state. He was followed by Scott Elliot (1894-95) and Moore (1900).

In 1905, the Englishman Douglas Freshfield climbed from the Uganda side. Responsible for many great feats on the Alps, he was and continued to be a dynamic explorer of mountains outside Europe. His numerous first ascents in the Caucasus mountains and his tour (in 1899) around Kangchenjunga are his greatest undertakings.

On Ruwenzori Freshfield failed. For a small expedition - Freshfield was accompanied by A.L Mumm and the Zermatt guide Moritz Inderblatten - the problems posed by the uninterrupted bad weather, storms and frequently zero visibility were too much. In 1906 the expedition organized and led by Louis Amedeus of Savoy, Duke of the Abruzzi was successful. Together with the Courmayeur guides Joseph Pétigax, César Ollier, Joseph Brocherel and Laurent Pétigax, the photographer Vittorio Sella and six other Italians, the descendant of the Savoy household faced the mountain with extreme resolution.

87

Leaving behind Sella and his assistants, entrusted with the task of recording the feat, he threw himself forward with the guides to take advantage of the smallest burst of good weather, the rarest asset on Ruwenzori. And he did it. At 9 a.m. on 21 June the leading rope party was below the last icy slopes of the highest peak. There was fog but Joseph Pétigax started to cut steps anyway, then aided by Ollier he overcame the vertical ledge. "Another few minutes and his Royal Highness set foot on the highest peak of the Ruwenzori range." All around, the horizon consisted in a uniform expanse of clouds from which "two white pyramids protruded sparkling in the sunlight: the extreme tips of the two highest peaks", as reads Filippo De Filippi's thrilling account. "His Royal Highness at that moment named [these] Margherita and Alexandra, so that, thanks to the patronage of the two sovereigns, the memory of the two nations would be

awkward. The paths are a series of muddy expanses and bogs, the refuge huts are rudimentary. There are visitors but nowhere near as many as the droves of trekkers encountered on the way to the Lenana Peak or Mount Kibo. Even the most adept traveller will find Ruwenzori a great, unforgettable adventure. Over the past few decades the two routes to the top have experienced alternating popularity. Just after the war, when Uganda was still the "pearl of Africa", most of the trekkers and mountaineers went up the Bujuku and Mobuku valleys, following the route taken by Freshfield and the Duke of the Abruzzi. In the years of Idi Amin's dictatorship and massacres, Uganda was closed to foreigners and the flow was diverted to the splendid Zaire region of Kivu and the steep path - that was first taken by Stuhlmann - that climbs from Mutwanga towards the glaciers and peaks. In the Nineties peace

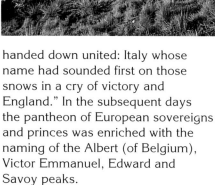

handed down united: Italy whose name had sounded first on those snows in a cry of victory and England." In the subsequent days the pantheon of European sovereigns and princes was enriched with the naming of the Albert (of Belgium), Victor Emmanuel, Edward and Savoy peaks. Today the times of the Duke and the Scramble for Africa may seem prehistory, yet of all the great mountains of Africa, Ruwenzori is the one that will take you back in time. Whatever side it is tackled from, the mountain is steep, discouraging,

returned to Uganda and the civil war in Rwanda sent hikers back to the eastern side. When it is possible to choose both ways have their attractions. The Zaire route is the most adventurous, taking you through the most humid and spectacular forests on the mountain and can be combined with one of the ascents to the Virunga volcanoes and an encounter with the gorillas in the Jomba forest. The journey from Goma to Beni and the base of the mountain is an adventure in itself on muddy and often interrupted roads.

From Uganda access is shorter but the path is equally difficult. The fact that a different route can be taken on the way down adds fascination to the trek on this side. Some groups stop at around 4,500 metres, at the base of the glaciers. Those with adequate experience and equipment should not miss the ascent to Pic Margherita - or at least to the 4,750 metres of the Stanley Plateau, dominated by the black Moebius rocks. Even lovelier, though today complicated by problems of visas, permits and logistics, is the crossing of the mountain. In this case the road

skirting the mountain to the south
allows a fast return to base.
In all cases, the botanic interest of
the Ruwenzori climb is extraordinary.
From the rainforest of the lower part
you pass to the magic world of
towering heather constantly
enveloped in cloud, then to the
senecious groundsel and giant
lobelias rising at around 4,000
metres. At the entrance to the
mountain forest, guides and porters
on both sides stop to pray and make
offerings to the gods. The remarkable
atmosphere of this mountain is
contagious for all visitors.

88 Beside the
Mahangu Hut
(3,310 metres)
a group of senecious
groundsel overlooks
the high altitude
steppe.

88-89 At about 3,000
metres, the path up
to Ruwenzori from
the Zaire side goes
through the beautiful,
shady forest of
arboreal heather.
Photographs by
Marco Majrani

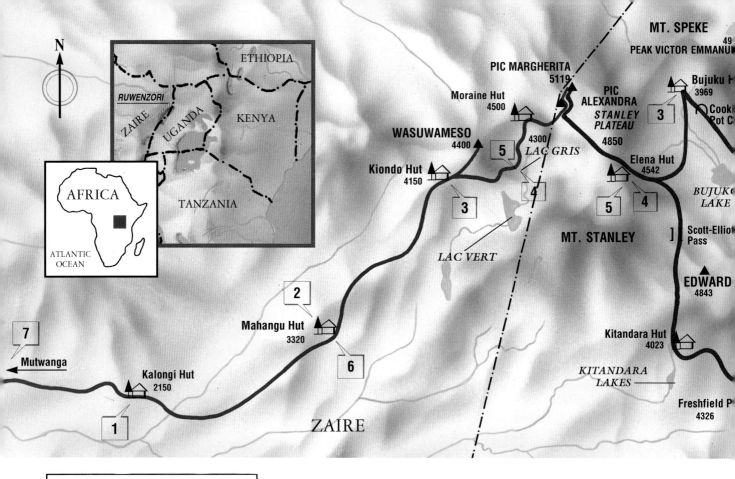

Labels on map:
ETHIOPIA
RUWENZORI
UGANDA
KENYA
ZAIRE
AFRICA
ATLANTIC OCEAN
TANZANIA

MT. SPEKE 49
PEAK VICTOR EMMANU
PIC MARGHERITA 5119
Moraine Hut 4500
PIC ALEXANDRA
STANLEY PLATEAU 4850
Bujuku H 3969
Cook Pot C
WASUWAMESO 4400
4300
LAC GRIS
3
Kiondo Hut 4150
5
Elena Hut 4542
BUJUK LAKE
3
4
LAC VERT
5
4
MT. STANLEY
Scott-Elliot Pass
EDWARD 4843
2
Mahangu Hut 3320
6
Kitandara Hut 4023
7
Mutwanga
Kalongi Hut 2150
KITANDARA LAKES
1
ZAIRE
Freshfield P 4326

USEFUL INFORMATION

Duration: 7 days for the Mutwanga route (Zaire), 8 for that from Ibanda (Uganda). Both times are reduced by 1-2 days for those stopping at the base of the glaciers but on both itineraries at least one extra day should be allowed for possible persistent bad weather.

Elevation: from 1,150 metres (Zaire) or 1,650 metres (Uganda) to 5,119 metres. The maximum altitude reached without setting foot on the glaciers is approximately 4,500 metres on both sides.

Period: the least rainy seasons (to call them "dry" would be a true exaggeration!) are between December and mid March and from June to September. On Ruwenzori it can rain at any time.

Red tape: a visa is needed both for Uganda and for Zaire. The permits required for the trek are obtained quickly and without problems at the base of the mountain. The cost of entry to the two national parks (Virunga National Park, Ruwenzori Mountain National Park) that protect the mountain is low.

Degree of difficulty: the paths on Ruwenzori are among the most awkward in the world because of the

boggy ground, the mud and the dense vegetation. But this is what makes a trek on the mountain an extraordinary adventure. Access to the Stanley Plateau glacier is easy from Uganda but steep and exposed to falling stones from Zaire. The final ascent to Pic Magherite includes passages on rock and rather steep glaciers, about AD.

Physical challenge: high because of the altitude, the ground and the climate.

Equipment: to the base of the glaciers normal trekking gear is sufficient. Ski sticks are extremely useful for balance on the mud and in the peat bogs. Your anorak and overtrousers must be of excellent quality and, above all, make sure that your changes of clothes are kept dry. Normal glacier gear is needed for the ascent to Pic Margherita with rope, ice axe, crampons, harness, some nails and ropes. On both treks a tent may be decidedly more comfortable than the refuge huts. These are small, often crowded and in poor condition and a tent is essential for a night at Lac Gris on the Zaire side.

Acess routes: Goma, the capital of eastern Zaire, is 2 hours' flight from the capital Kinshasa. The traditional and fast access from Kigali, capital of Rwanda, will not be possible again until peace is restored in the country. The 400 kilometres of dirt track between Goma and Beni takes 15-20 hours: by plane it takes just one. From Beni another 50 kilometres of trail, 2-3 hours, will take you to the village of Mutwanga (1,150 metres).
Nearby, at Mutsora, are the offices of the "Ruwenzori section" of the Virunga National Park. Access from Uganda is simpler: 7-8 hours suffice to cover the 411 kilometres of asphalt road between Kampala and Kasese from where you come quickly to Ibanda and the start of the Nyakalengija path. There are also regular flights between Kampala and Kasese.
The Kampala-Kasese railway is picturesque but very slow.

Guides and porters: on both sides porters can be hired rapidly and without difficulty at the base of the mountain. The charges are very low. In Zaire it is obligatory to be

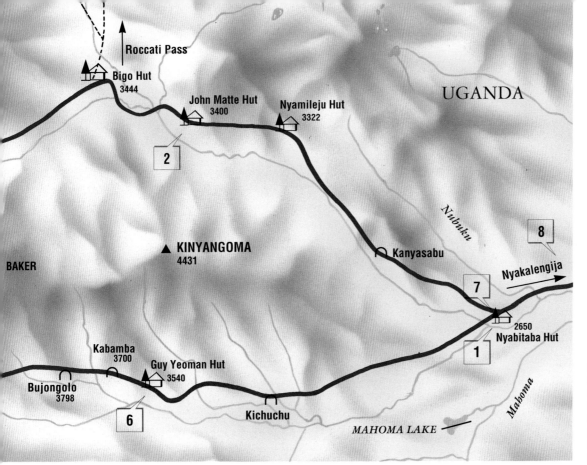

Roccati Pass

Bigo Hut
3444

John Matte Hut
3400

Nyamileju Hut
3322

UGANDA

2

Nubuku

8

KINYANGOMA
4431

Kanyasabu

BAKER

Nyakalengija

7

Nyabitaba Hut
2650

Kabamba
3700

Guy Yeoman Hut
3540

1

Bujongolo
3798

Kichuchu

Mahoma

6

MAHOMA LAKE

91 top The humid and misty high altitude steppes are crossed by the tiring but fascinating paths leading to the Mount Stanley glaciers.

accompanied by a Park ranger (his board is paid by the trekker). From the Zaire side a programme for the professional training of guides capable of taking clients to Pic Margherita was started in 1990 but abandoned before the end of the course. Those who participated are capable of tackling rocks and glaciers. On the Uganda side contact the Rwenzori Mountaineering Service.

Detours and peaks: unlike Kilimanjaro and Mount Kenya, Ruwenzori is a proper mountain chain comprising six massifs. Among the secondary peaks, the most popular are the easy Moebius (4,900 metres), the graceful Pic Alexandra (5,097 metres), flanking the highest peak and, above all, the Victor Emmanuel peak (4,901 metres), the highest on Mount Speke, reached from Bujuku Hut on the route from Uganda.

In case of trouble: there are no mountain rescue services. The isolation of Ruwenzori and awkward paths make the transfer down to the valley of any injured persons difficult. The fairly steep paths make it easy to descend

quickly in the event of mountain sickness.

Maps: the best are those published by the Department of Land and Surveys of Uganda. Ruwenzori is included on the sheets 1:50,000 *65/The Margherita* and *66/The Mobuku* and the 1:25,000 *Central Ruwenzori sheet.*

Guidebooks: There is the *Guide to the Ruwenzori* by H.A. Osmaston and D. Pasteur (Mountain Club of Uganda, 1972), *Trekking in East Africa* by David Else (Lonely Planet, 1993) or *Backpacker's Africa - East and Southern* by Hilary Bradt (Bradt-Hunter, 1989).

For further reading the story of the first ascent to the peaks of the mountain is contained in *Ruwenzori* (Hoepli, 1908) officially by the Duke of the Abruzzi but actually written by Filippo de Filippi and with splendid photographs by Vittorio Sella. Also of interest is the chapter on Ruwenzori in *Snowcaps on the Equator* by Clive Ward, Gordon Boy and Iain Allan (The Bodley Head, 1988).

91 bottom The forest of arboreal heather is one of the most surprising sights on Ruwenzori. The photograph

shows a party on the Zaire side, between the Mahangu and Kyondo huts. Photographs by Marco Majrani

THE ROUTE FROM ZAIRE

FIRST DAY
from Mutwanga to the Kalongi Hut
distance climbed: 1,100 metres
distance descended: 100 metres
time: 5 hours

Rather long but not too tiring, the first stage poses the odd problem at the beginning; it is exposed to the sun and because of the necessary preparations must be followed when the sun is high. From the village of Mutwanga follow the good path up the slopes covered with elephant grass passing numerous peasant huts and leading (1,600 metres) to the edge of a splendid tropical mountain forest. There is a long series of zigzags passing numerous streams. After a long stretch of continuous but fairly easy climb you will reach the large terrace and the Kalongi Hut (2,150 metres).

92 top A ranger in the Virunga National Park stops amid the giant heathers that surround the path to Ruwenzori between the Kalongi and Mahangu Huts.
Photograph by Marco Majrani

92 centre On the way from the Mahangu Hut to the Kiondo Hut, at approximately 3,500 metres, the *heather forest ends and you step into the world of senecious groundsel.*
Photograph by Marco Majrani

92 bottom Two trekkers arrive at the Kalongi Hut (2750 metres), the first on the Ruwenzori route from the Zairese side.
Photograph by Stefano Ardito

93 top Built in wood at the times of the Belgian administration, the Mahangu Hut stands on a lovely grassy terrace at 3,320 metres. Photograph by Stefano Ardito

93 centre top A party of trekkers on the charming path through senecious groundsel that leads to the Mahangu Hut. Photograph by Stefano Ardito

93 centre bottom Surrounded by a thick forest of groundsel, Lac Vert (4200 metres) is one of the loveliest on Ruwenzori and is passed before the start of the climb to the top of Mount Stanley. Photograph by Marco Majrani

93 bottom At the end of the third day trekkers stop at the Kiondo Hut (4,200 metres), built on a grassy ridge. The peaks of Mount Speke appear in the backfground immersed in clouds. Photograph by Stefano Ardito

SECOND DAY
*from the Kalongi Hut
to Mahangu Hut
distance climbed: 1,160 metres
time: 4 hours*

A long and tiring stage on which the path climbs almost without interruption to the magnificent natural terrace and the Mahangu Hut, within sight of the Mount Stanley peaks. Start with a brief stretch across the mountain, beyond which the path reaches and follows a steep ridge surrounded by woods. After about an hour the porters will stop to make offerings to the mountain gods. Then you start climbing again up the still steep and increasingly muddy path, through beautiful giant heather "trees" and thick blankets of moss until you come out on the Mahangu shelf (3,320 metres). From here, the porters must descend almost 150 metres on a steep muddy path to procure water.

THIRD DAY
*from the Mahangu Hut
to Kyondo Hut
distance climbed: 840 metres
time: 3-4 hours 30 minutes*

Shorter and not so steep as the previous day, this is when the altitude starts to make itself felt. Trained parties heading for the peaks can continue the same day for the lakes; otherwise it is advisable to climb up and admire the sunset from the Wasuwameso Ridge. After leaving Mahangu, the path climbs through the last heathers and then proceeds through senecious groundsel and lobelias, crossing various areas of boggy terrain. A steeper climb leads to the Kyondo Hut (4,150 metres, 3 hours) which, unlike the previous ones, is built in stone. From here a clear path continues amid stones and vegetation to the Wasuwameso peak (4,400 metres, 1-1 hour 30 minutes return).

FOURTH DAY

*from the Kyondo Hut to Lac Gris
distance climbed: 300 metres
distance descended: 150 metres
time: 2 hours*

A short stage that the groups not intending to tackle the glacier can combine with an initial descent. In case of rain some stretches of the crossing require care. After leaving Kyondo the path crosses the steep slopes of Wasuwameso where some passages on often muddy rocks call for attention. Some sturdy, well fixed ropes are mixed with others that are not very reliable. At the end of the crossing a path through lobelias and senecious groundsel zigzags, offering a perfect view of the beautiful Lac Vert and then climbs to the banks of Lac Gris

(4,300 metres) where you camp within sight of the steep slopes of Mount Stanley. It is possible to complete the day by climbing to the old and no longer used Moraine Hut (4,500 metres, 1-1 hour 30 minutes return) on a scenic and windy saddle.

FIFTH DAY

*from Lac Gris
to Pic Margherita and back
distance climbed and descended:
800 metres
time: 8-10 hours*

Free from true difficulties but on delicate terrain, the climb to the highest peak on Ruwenzori is only for mountaineers. The difficulty varies greatly according to the conditions. An hour on a semi-path on screes and then through large morainic blocks will take you to the base of the Stanley Glacier. This is tackled via a steep slope (50°, difficult if ice is fresh) proceeding then along broad slopes at the foot of the south face of Pic Alexandra to the Stanley Plateau (4,850 metres). Cross this downwards to the foot of the Alexandra rocks and climb for a stretch up the icy ravine between the two peaks. At the end you can choose between the summit

decorated with the characteristic "cauliflowers" of ice that leads directly to Margherita (traditional route but increasingly more difficult as the snowline retreats) or the ascent between the two main peaks followed by a short but steep climb to the 5,119 metres of the summit. Descend by the same way: beware of falling stones and ice that the sun may detach from the south face of Pic Alexandra.

SIXTH DAY

from Lac Gris to the Mahangu Hut
distance climbed: 100 metres
distance descended: 1,250 metres
time: 5 hours

Leaving the moraine at the base of Mount Stanley, cross back to the Kyondo Hut and proceed down to the Mahangu Hut, thus having a last glance at the sunset towards the highest peaks on Ruwenzori. Descend via the same path used for the ascent to Mahangu.

SEVENTH DAY

from Mahangu Hut to Mutwanga
distance climbed: 100 metres
distance descended: 2,260 metres
time: 6 hours 30 minutes

Rather tiring for the steep and muddy terrain, the last day of the trek leads you back to the forest and the inhabited world. The route is the same as on the way up, the most tiring stretch being that across the forest after the Kalongi Hut because of the short but tiring climbs.

THE ROUTE FROM UGANDA

96 top left The first section of the path follows the clear water of the Mubuku river which collects the waters of the eastern side of Ruwenzori.

96 bottom left A party of trekkers descending from Freshfield Pass in the wild Mobuku river valley, along the path explored in 1906 by the Duke of the Abruzzi and his Aosta Valley guides.

FIRST DAY
*from Nyakalengija
to the Nyabitaba Hut
distance climbed: 1,000 metres
time: 5 hours*

A rather long and quite tiring stage introducing you to the splendid forests on the Ugandan side of Ruwenzori. Start beside the small

plantations of beans, bananas and coffee and proceed in the elephant grass. Enter the forest and continue along the clear waters of the Mobuku river with numerous zigzags on slippery terrain. After crossing two streams, proceed almost on the flat for more than an hour, cross Lake Mahoma and then climb up a steep ridge to the Nyabitaba Hut (2,650 metres), restored in the early Nineties. Before the hut you will pass the small altars erected by the local hunters and porters in honour of the Ruwenzori gods. There is also a large, natural shelter shortly before the building.

SECOND DAY

from the Nyabitaba Hut
to the John Matte Hut
distance climbed: 850 metres
distance descended: 100 metres
time: 6 hours

As on the Zaire side, the stage
in the forest of heather and moss
is the most tiring of the trek.
Start from the ridge, descend
steeply to the Mobuku river, crossed
on a new, convenient suspended
bridge (the previous bridge was
periodically washed away by the
floods). Continue on a steep section
before an hour's easier hike through
bamboos, passing beside the
natural shelter of Kanyasabu.
Last comes a long and awkward

THIRD DAY

from the John Matte Hut
to the Bujuku Hut
distance climbed: 750 metres
distance descended: 100 metres
time: 5 hours

A long stage with a limited climb
but on particularly difficult terrain:
you cross the two tremendous peat
bogs that precede and follow Bigo
Hut. Continue following the river,
cross a lovely scenic part of the
heather forest and proceed on open
land to the Lower Bigo Bog.
Once across the river, continue
as best as you can to the Bigo Hut
(3,444 metres) where the path for
the pass that separates Mount Emin
from Mount Gessi branches off to

the right (north). The main route
follows the base of the rocky slopes
of Mount Stanley, crosses the Upper
Bigo Bog (or Kibatsi Bog), skirts
the lovely Bujuku Lake to Cooking
Pot Cave (or Bujuku Cave) and
climbs to the Bujuku Hut (3,962
metres). From here you can devote
a day to climbing the Victor
Emmanuel Peak (4,901 metres,
PD, 8 hours return), the highest
on Mount Speke.

climb on muddy terrain around
large rocks. Once in the heather
forest, you will soon come to the
Nyamileju Hut (3,322 metres),
in a sorry state, beside which there
is another large cave. A last hour's
hike leads to the new and
comfortable John Matte Hut
(3,400 metres).

97 left Convenient
recently built metal
bridges allow
today's trekker to
avoid the awkward
and dangerous fords
of the Mobuku river.

97 top right
Two trekkers cross
the Upper Bigo Bog
(3,500 metres), one
of the most difficult
bogs on the path
on the Ugandan
side of Ruwenzori.

97 right bottom
Between Cooking
Pot Cave and Lake
Bujuku, at about
3,800 metres above
sea level, the path
to the Bujuku Hut
branches off that
to the Elena Hut
and Mount Stanley.
Photographs by
Cl. Jaccoux/
Agence Freestyle

96 top right
The road between
Ibanda and
Nyakalengija and
the path climbing
the Ugandan side
of Ruwenzori wind
through cultivated
fields and orchards.

96 bottom right
At the lower edge
of the Ruwenzori
forest the Ugandan
peasants often use
fire to increase the
size of their fields.

FOURTH DAY
from Bujuku Hut to Elena Hut
distance climbed: 550 metres
time: 3 hours

Overlooking the glaciers of Mount Stanley, the small Elena refuge hut marks the highest accessible point on the Uganda side of Ruwenzori for those who do not wish to tackle the glaciers. Those not trying for the top can go to the refuge hut and proceed

on the same day towards Kitandara: the porters descend to spend the night at Bukuju. Start by returning to Cooking Pot Cave from where the path rises up a steep canal between rocks and groundsel with easy rock passages, one of which equipped with metal steps. Before reaching Scott-Elliot Pass climb crossways to the right at the foot of a band of rocks, pass alongside the dry walls of the last 1906 camp and continue amid sheet rock and screes to the Elena Hut (4,542 metres), a short distance from the glacier.

FIFTH DAY
from Elena Hut
to Pic Margherita and back
distance climbed: 720 metres
time: 6-8 hours

The climb from Uganda to the highest peak of Ruwenzori is a little easier and shorter than that on the Zaire side. From the refuge hut, reach and climb the easy slopes of the eastern Stanley glacier, keeping to the right (east) to avoid some large crevices. After coming without difficulty to Stanley Plateau, the wide saddle (4,850 metres) between Pic Alexandra and the Moebius peak, continue on the route already described to Pic Margherita (5,119 metres). The descent is by the same way.

SIXTH DAY

from Elena Hut to Guy Yeoman Hut
distance climbed: 400 metres
distance descended: 1200 metres
time: 7 hours

A long and extremely interesting stage on which you pass the Bujongolo cave, where the Duke of the Abruzzi's expedition established its base camp. This stage can be split and a night spent beside the magnificent twin lakes of Kitandra, dominated by the Mount Baker massif in one of the most spectacular and wildest corners of Ruwenzori. Start along the outward path and then branch right (south) to Scott-Elliot Pass (4,327 metres), from where you descend southwards to the foot of the Mount Baker buttress and the first of the two magnificent Kitandara lakes. Go round this and you will soon come to Kitandara Hut (4,023 metres) beside the second lake. A steep and tiring climb leads to Freshfield Pass (4,326 metres) from where you descend steeply into the head of the Mobuku Valley. After crossing a secondary ridge, descend to the Bujongolo (3,798 metres) and Kabamba (3,700 metres) caves, to the lovely Kabamba falls and the new Guy Yeoman Hut (3,540 metres).

SEVENTH DAY

from Guy Yeoman Hut
to Nyabitaba Hut
distance descended: 950 metres
time: 5 hours

A rather long stage, descending into the deep and wild Mobuku valley which includes a number of steep, exposed and slippery stretches in descent that call for care. If the river level is high this stretch may become impossible. Start with an initial steep and muddy section, passing to the right of the river at Buamba (3,518 metres) and then descending again steeply beside the river, overcoming some short exposed passages to the clearing and the barely adequate rocky shelter of Kichuchu, at the end of the trickiest stretch. An easier descent through bamboos leads to another ford on the Mobuku river (3,200 metres). A long and less tiring stretch on a ridge precedes the final descent to the Nyabitaba Hut.

EIGHTH DAY

from the Nyabitaba Hut
to Nyakalengija
distance descended: 1,000 metres
time: 3 hours

The last stage in the trek retraces the outward route on the right bank of the Mobuku river to the fields, plantations and the road.

99 top right
Between the Guy Yeoman and the Nyabitaba Huts the Mobuku Valley path presents a number of slippery and sometimes delicate passages.

99 bottom right
Two trekkers on a muddy ridge at the foot of a rock face on the Mobuku Valley path.
Photographs by Cl. Jaccoux/ Agence Freestyle

98 top left The path climbing to the Elena Hut crosses a harsh, wild rocky landscape.

98 bottom left Before the Scott-Eliott Pass the path up to Mount Stanley goes through a splendid forest of groundsel.

98 top right Two trekkers climb one of the metal ladders between the Bujuku and Elena Huts.

98 bottom right The Elena Hut (4,500 metres) is the starting point for the ascent to Stanley Plateau and the Margherita and Alexandra peaks.

99 top left At about 4,000 metres, at the head of the Mobuku Valley the path comes to the two lovely Kitandara lakes.

99 bottom left A trekker on the steep path down from Freshfield Pass towards the Bujongolo and Kabamba caves-refuges, the Kabamba Falls and the Guy Yeoman Hut.

VIRUNGA: THE GORILLAS' VOLCANOES

Lava, forests and great apes
on the border between Zaire, Rwanda and Uganda

"Every twitch of anger was followed by a brief moment of calm. Brown or blue, the smoke rose in heavy spirals, while a deafening roar, similar to that of a monstrous hound, rocked the volcano. The nerves had no time to relax, so close was another sudden tremor, another explosion, the return of the incandescence, the start of a new volley. The bombs of lava rose with a drone."

Thus, in the spring of 1948 did Haroun Tazieff, one of the most famous volcanologists of all times, describe the eruption of Kituro, a volcanic cone opened a few weeks earlier at the foot of Nyamulagira and Nyiragongo, within sight of the northern bank of Lake Kivu in the Congo, later to become Zaire. *Cratères en feu*, the book published in 1951 telling of the adventurous African explorations is still an all-time classic of volcanology.

The fascination of the volcanoes rising to mark the edge of Rift Valley amidst the great forests on the border between Uganda, Rwanda and Zaire is not created by the eruptions alone. The 3,462 metres of Nyiragongo dominate the skyline of Goma, the capital of eastern Zaire, and the tranquil landscape of the banks of the lake. The path climbing the slopes is the busiest in the area and after five hours' climb you can look over an impressive caldera more than half a kilometre wide, protected by vertical walls almost 200 metres high and often illuminated by incandescent flowing lava.

Farther north in the forests of the Virunga National Park Nyamulagira is lower - it measures a "mere" 3,062 metres in height - less visible and more active. The main crater is reached after roughly one and a half days' march from the road between Goma, Rwindi and Beni and offers another impressive spectacle. On the sides of the volcano are a series of adventitious cones, clefts,

and dried-up lava flows, telling a story of eruptions and explosions that has by no means ended.

The last outburst of activity, that of Kitzangurwa, was in July 1986. Nine years earlier, in 1977, the lava of Rugarambiro killed hundreds of people in the nearby villages.

In Kinyarwanda, one of the most widely spoken local languages, the name Virunga - meaning "place with fire", "cooking pot", "he who cooks" - is applied to all the mountains of volcanic origin. Inevitably the whole volcanic region north of Lake Kivu has been given this name. East of Nyiragongo and the Kibati road pass, the chain continues with peaks that have for many centuries been volcanically inactive on the surface. Their altitude, beauty and the dense forest covering their slopes make

them more particularly attractive destinations.

The most spectacular, Mikeno, stands entirely in Zaire and overlooks the Goma-Beni road, made by the Belgians in the Thirties. Rising to 4,437 metres and named the "Matterhorn of Africa" by various explorers (Mikeno in Kinyarwanda means "the desolate") it has attracted the attention of explorers and mountaineers since the late nineteenth century. In the Twenties King Albert of Belgium, famous for his mountain ascents, had to give up on the slopes of Mikeno.

The first to reach the summit, in 1927, was father Van Hoef of the nearby Lulenga mission. Twenty years later the Canadian mountaineer Earl Denman arrived in the area.

100 The Sabinyo peak (3,634 metres), in local dialect "the father with large teeth", is one of the most spectacular and wildest in Virunga.
Photograph by Geoffrey Roy/ Agence Freestyle

101 An encounter with a silverback, the adult male mountain gorilla is the most exciting moment on a trek on Virunga.
Photograph by Camerapix

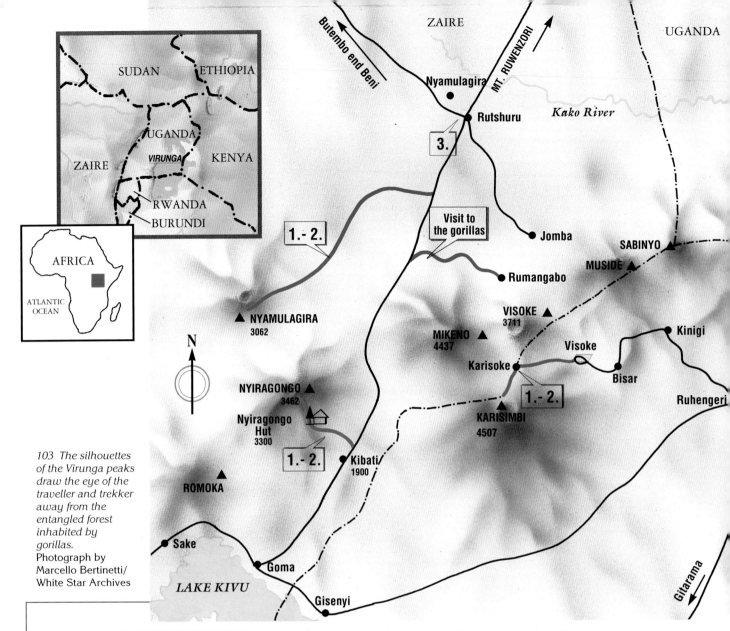

103 The silhouettes of the Virunga peaks draw the eye of the traveller and trekker away from the entangled forest inhabited by gorillas. Photograph by Marcello Bertinetti/White Star Archives

USEFUL INFORMATION

Duration: the Nyiragongo ascent takes two days, that to Nyamulagira three. The visit to the gorillas is completed in a day's hike from Jomba.

Elevation: from 1,600 to 4,507 metres

Period: the least wet seasons are from December to mid-March and from June to September.
On the Virunga mountains, as well as on the nearby Ruwenzori, it can however rain at any time of the year. Karisimbi, in particular, is known for its sudden icy storms.

Red tape: a visa is required for all three countries. The permits needed for the ascent to the Nyiragongo and Nyamulagira summits are obtained quickly and without difficulty in the Virunga National Park Offices, those for the Parc National des Volcans (Rwanda) at Ruhengeri. Access to the Bwindi National Park and the Kiezi

Gorilla Sanctuary (both in Uganda) is strictly controlled. A visit to the gorillas must always be booked some time in advance.

Difficulties: there are no technical problems but great attention must be paid to eruptions in course, especially on Nyamulagira.

Physical challenge: average.

Equipment: normal hiking gear. The rudimentary refuge huts on Nyamulagira and Nyiragongo make a tent unnecessary although one is recommended on Karisimbi. Everywhere you will need a mattress, sleeping bag and good protection against the rain.

Access routes: Goma, the capital of eastern Zaire, is two hours by plane from the capital of Kinshasa, or by land across the border with Rwanda. Ruhengeri, at the foot of the Rwandan side of the volcanoes, is 90 kilometres from the capital Kigali. Access from the Rwandan side will of course only be possible and recommended after peace has

returned to this country.
From Goma a good dirt track leads in 13 kilometres to Kibati and in 70 kilometres to Rutshuru where there is a turn for Jomba and Nymulagira. From Ruhengeri it is a short journey to Kinigi, Bisate and the Visoke entrance to the Volcans National Park.

Guides and porters: hikes on the Zaire and Rwandan side of Virunga can only be made if you are accompanied by the rangers of one of the two parks. Porters can also be hired. Visits to the gorillas are made in small parties and members must maintain total silence.

Detours and peaks: from the Rwandan side fairly good paths in the thick forest permit an ascent to Visoke (3,711 metres), Sabinyo (3,634 metres), Muhavura (4,227 metres) and Mgahinga (3,474 metres). The ascent of Mikeno (4,437 metres) on the Zaire side is the most demanding in the area.

▲ KAMENA HILL
2367

LAKE
— MUTANDA

▲ KASOONI HILL
2260

LAKE
TSHAHAFI

LAKE
MUGISHA

MUHAVURA ▲

GAHINGA
474

LAKE
BULERA —

LAKE
LUHONDO

Kigali

RWANDA

In case of trouble: the treks are short and this permits a fairly fast return to the road and civilization. There is an excellent hospital at Goma built with Italian state collaboration.
Maps: there are no detailed maps.
Guidebooks: *Backpacker's Africa - East and Southern* by Hilary Bradt (Bradt-Hunter, 1989).
For further reading: Haroun Tazieff, the great French volcanologist has devoted fascinating pages to the volcanoes of Kivu. Among these *Cratères en Feu* (Arthaud, 1951), *Nyiragongo ou le volcan interdit* (Flammarion, 1975) and the autobiography *Le Vagabond des volcans* (2 volumes, Stock, 1991). To learn more about the gorillas and Dian Fossey's adventure, the best read is *Gorillas in the Mist* (Hodder & Stoughton, 1983). Also of interest *Snowcaps on the Equator* by Iain Allan, Gordon Boy and Clive Ward (The Bodley Head, 1989) and *Africa's Mountains of the Moon* by Guy Yeoman (Elm Tree Books, 1989).

He was to become famous for his attempt to climb Everest in 1947 with an expedition of just three people. One after the other, he reached all eight of these main volcanoes. On the very steep slopes of mud, rock and vegetation of Mikeno Denman climbed "in the simplest way possible always barefoot, groping in the mist and rain dressed only in a pair of shorts and a threadbare shirt."
East of Mikeno, the equally wild Sabinyo (3,634 metres), the "old man with large teeth" for the locals, marks the point where Zaire, Rwanda and Uganda meet. Even farther east, between Rwanda and Uganda, stand Mgahinga (3,474 metres) and Muhavura (4,227 metres) sighted in 1861 by the Speke and Grant expedition heading for Lake Victoria. Poised on the border between Zaire and Rwanda are Visoke (3,711 metres) with a beautiful lake on its summit and the mighty Karisimbi, at 4,507 metres the highest Virunga peak and the sixth highest of the great African mountains after Kilimanjaro, Kenya, Ruwenzori, Ras Dashan and Meru.
The most fascinating and rarest animals in Africa and indeed the whole planet can be seen on the slopes of Karisimbi and Sabinyo. Extremely strong, grand, perfectly adjusted to the impenetrable habitat of the Virunga forests, this gorilla (the scientific name is *Gorilla gorilla beringei*) was only discovered in 1902 by the engineer Oscar Beringe and few more than 300 specimens, equally divided among the three countries, have survived to the present day. In 1959 two outstanding American scholars started to bring the mountain gorilla and its fight for survival to the attention of the rest of the world.
The first, George Schaller, studied this animal between 1959 and 1962; he accustomed some gorilla families to the presence of man and let out a cry of alarm against the increasingly widespread poaching. Inspired by Schaller's books and conferences, in 1967 the Californian Dian Fossey left her work in the USA for the Virunga slopes. Her first six months of work on the slopes of Mikeno were interrupted by the civil war in the Congo. After moving to Rwanda she stayed for the next thirteen years at Karisoke, an

outcrop of buildings on the saddle between Karisimbi and Mikeno.
As her friendship with the great apes became firmer, her cries in defence of this magnificent species became louder year after year - and were recorded in America and Europe by National Geographic and in the book *Gorillas in the Mist.*
On December 27th 1987, on her return from an umpteenth round of conferences, Dian Fossey was assassinated at Karisoke in circumstances that remain mysterious. At her explicit request she was buried in the small local cemetery close to her beloved gorillas. Partially and mainly thanks to her courageous battle - in 1988 *Gorillas in the Mist* became a successful film interpreted by Sigourney Weaver - increasing numbers of tourists approach the difficult paths of the rainforest to observe these extraordinary animals. Unfortunately, the political vicissitudes of the three Virunga countries are of no help to the survival of the species.
An encounter with the families of gorillas in the thick forest particularly the silverbacks, adult males weighing almost two hundred kilos, is one of the most exciting of my personal experiences in the Parks and on the mountains of this entire planet.

THE VISIT TO THE GORILLAS

ONE-DAY TREK
From Jomba or Rumangabo

There are two starting bases for a visit to the gorilla forest on the Zaire side. The best known and most popular, Jomba, is reached along a track for 4x4 vehicles and has a comfortable lodge and small Park visitor centre. In the forest the walk in search of the gorillas usually lasts between 2 and 4 hours. Rumangabo is 4 hours hike along a pleasant path: again it is difficult to predict the length of the march in the forest. The visit is open to limited numbers in both areas.

NYIRAGONGO

FIRST DAY
from Kibati to the Nyiragongo Hut
distance climbed: 1,400 metres
time: 4 hours 30 minutes

The forceful silhouette of Nyiragongo dominates Goma and the northern bank of Lake Kivu. To reach the path that climbs to the mountain follow the road to Rwindi, Butembo and Beni as far as the sparse houses of Kibati (1,900 metres, 13 kilometres from the town) where you can hire a guide and porters if desired and complete the few bureaucratic formalities. Then take the path opened after much *panga* work (the African version of the machete) crossing a cultivated area and entering the forest; this rises slowly towards the mountain. After passing an area of fumaroles, steeper slopes lead to two metal huts (3,300 metres) a short distance from the crater.

104 top Built by
the Belgians in the
Thirties, the road
that links Goma with
Rwindi, Butembo
and Beni is often in

a very sorry state
because of the mud
and landslides.
Photograph by
Geoffrey Roy/
Agence Freestyle

104 centre
A party of trekkers
passes through the
thick and
spectacular forest
in the Volcans

National Park on
the Rwandan side
of Virunga.
Photograph by
Geoffrey Roy/
Agence Freestyle

104 bottom
At about 3,000
metres the path that
climbs from Kibati
and the Goma-Beni
road towards the

Nyiragongo crater
passes through a
lovely fumarole
area.
Photograph by
Stefano Ardito

SECOND DAY
from the Hut
to the Nyiragongo crater and Kibati
distance climbed: 100 metres
distance descended: 1,550 metres
time: 4 hours

The climb from the huts to the
crater takes half an hour. In the
event of an eruption this should be
done by night to admire the
extraordinary spectacle of the
flowing lava on the bottom of the
crater. The edge of the crater can be
followed partially: the complete tour
around this includes some aerial
and awkward sections and takes
1 hour 30 minutes. The descent is
along the same path as the ascent
and leads quickly to Kibati.

104-105 A trekker
looks down onto the
impressive
Nyiragongo crater
(3,462 metres).
Photograph by
Stefano Ardito

106 top Part of the gorillas' diet, the bamboo that grows on the Virunga slopes will be of interest to botany enthusiasts.
Photograph by David Keith Jones/ Image of Africa Photobank

106 top centre Before plunging into the forest, the paths from Rwanda, Zaire and Uganda pass through a series of small clearings.
Photograph by David Keith Jones/ Image of Africa Photobank

106 centre bottom Large, fast and aggressive, the buffalo is met fairly often in the Virunga forests. If this occurs the trekker must act with the utmost caution.
Photograph by S. Gurzynski/ Agence Freestyle

106 bottom The trek passes through small clearings surrounded by thick vegetation where groups of nimble antelopes can be sighted.
Photograph by Stefano Ardito

NYAMULAGIRA

FIRST DAY
from Rutshuru
to the Nyamulagira Hut
distance climbed: 1,100 metres
distance descended: 100 metres
time: 6 hours

The path into the forest towards the foot of the volcano starts at a height of 1,500 metres, about 10 kilometres south of Rutshuru, on the track to Goma. The route, highly attractive and always varied, leads to the crossing of a series of lava flows and wide clearings where antelopes, chimpanzees, buffaloes and elephants can be sighted. The "hut" is in actual fact a large, comfortable brick building approximately 2,500 metres above sea-level and quite welcoming although the conditions are far from excellent.

SECOND DAY
from the Hut
to the Nyamulagira crater and back
distance climbed: 600 metres
time: 4 hours

Leaving the hut behind you, proceed in the forest along a muddier path than that of the previous day. After about an hour you will come out of the high trunk vegetation and continue on open rocky ground to the crater lip (3,000 metres approximately); here you can look over the impressive, wide, flat Nyamulagira caldera, rich in bizarre rock formations, fumaroles and areas of vegetation. The guide will indicate the best route to follow inside the crater. The return to the refuge hut is by the same way.

THIRD DAY
from the Nyamulagira Hut
to Rutshuru
distance climbed: 100 metres
distance descended: 1,100 metres
time: 4 hours

The trek from the refuge hut to the Goma-Beni road follows the same path as on the outward journey. It is a little quicker. The landscape, fauna and flora make this day as fascinating as the others.

107 top left
A party of trekkers on a stretch where the thick vegetation and high grass can create more than a little difficulty.
Photograph by Marcello Bertinetti/ White Star Archives

107 bottom left
The small clearings that break up the dense forest are where gorillas are most commonly sighted.
Photograph by Stefano Ardito

KARISIMBI

FIRST DAY
from the Visoke entrance
to the Lukumi Refuge
distance climbed: 1,400 metres
time: 5 hours

The paths towards Lake Ngezi, the Mikeno peak and Karisimbi start from the vast clearing (approximately 2,400 metres) where the road ends. Follow the track entering the dense forest to climb a marked rocky ravine surrounded by thick bamboo, hagenia and hypericum forest and then continue to the saddle (3,000 metres approximately) between Karisimbi and Visoke where the buildings of the Karisoke Study Centre and Dian Fossey's grave are situated. Branch left (south) and proceed along the narrow path rising in the forest again to the small and poorly kept Lukumi Refuge (3,800 metres approximately) at the foot of the steep, stony slopes that lead to the peak.

SECOND DAY
from the Lukumi Refuge
to Karisimbi and the Visoke entrance
distance climbed: 700 metres
distance descended: 2,100 metres
time: 7 hours 30 minutes

The route from the refuge hut to the peak, all on open ground covered with lobelia, poses no problems except those caused by the far from infrequent bad weather. In about two hours you will reach the wide Karisimbi summit (4,507 metres), one of the best scenic spots on the continent, though unfortunately an antenna and various other things (anything but in keeping with the beauty of the place) lessen the effect somewhat. The descent by the same route will take little more than 1 hour to the refuge hut and 4 hours from it to the entrance to the Volcans National Park.

107 right
A silverback observes the photographer in the Virunga forest. These splendid creatures can weigh up to 160 kilograms but pose no threat to man.
Photograph by David Keith Jones/ Image of Africa Photobank

THE ABERDARES

Through the dense Kikuyu forests

The Kikuyu plateau, 20 September 1899. One week after conquering the Batian peak, Halford Mackinder's caravan started on the way back to Nairobi from where he would travel by train to Mombasa and the coast. The Scottish mountaineer was not yet satisfied with his journey and wanted to follow a partially different itinerary. So after emerging from the forest of Mount Kenya the caravan headed towards another chain of mountains, not so high but mantled with splendid forests. "We were in a rolling, green land, with winding, wooded valleys" recorded Mackinder in his diary. "A landscape that were it not for the bright red ground could have been that of the English Downs. The rock was volcanic but as soft as chalk, the trees gripping the rocks were like those of Mount Kenya and they were blanketed with moss. The wind blew constantly from the east and drove the clouds towards the Sattima summit."

By one of the many ironies of the geography of the continent, the Aberdares - a chain named after a Welsh lord president of the Royal Geographical Society - are one of the most authentic areas of the Kenyan highlands and of all the mountains in Africa. Not so high and less spectacular than the Batian and the nearby peaks, the extinct volcanoes that form this chain are covered with dense forest and host a fauna of great interest. Those following the road from Nairobi northwards will see to the left "the dark horizon of the Kikuyu forests" that a hundred years ago attracted Mackinder's attention. Those following the paths towards Shipton's Caves, Teleki Valley and the peaks of Mount Kenya can, in the terse light of morning, see in detail the highest peaks of the Aberdares and the whole silhouette of the chain that the Kikuyu call Nyandarua, "the skin stretched out to dry".

108 The Saliente forests in the eastern sector of the Park are the thickest on the range; they are home to a varied fauna including elephants, black rhinoceros and lions.

108-109 Situated on the Aberdares slopes, the spectacular Thompson's Falls are the most popular and photographed in Africa.
Photographs by David Keith Jones/ Images of Africa Photobank

110-111
The Aberdares
forests offer some
of the best
opportunities in all
eastern Africa for
the sighting of wild
animals. Here can be
seen a cow elephant
and her calf.
Photograph by
Carla Signorini
Jones/Images of
Africa Photobank

To the north rises solitary Oldoinyo Lesatima (4,000 metres), the highest peak of the massif, the "Mountain of the Young Bull" for the Masai. To the south, beyond the Table Mountain (3,790 metres) and the Rurimueria Hill (3,886 metres) stands Kinangop (3,906 metres), a corruption of Ilkinaapop, "the Lords of the Earth" in the tongue of the Purko, a Masai clan that fought in ferocious skirmishes with the Kikuyu. Closing the list is the Elephant (3,591 metres), lower but singular in shape.

On the opposite side the chain descends steeply to the deep Rift and the Naivasha and Nakuru lakes, famous for their thousands of flamingoes. The Aberdares are also a nature paradise. The dense forest covering the slopes of the mountains is home to buffalo,

volcanic rock. On a clear day the peaks offer stunning views of Mount Kenya, rising majiestic and streaked with ice beyond the plateau.

The first European to sight the chain was the Englishman Joseph Thomson, who in 1883 crossed the Nanyuki and Nyeri plateau and named the mountains after the patron of his journey.

Sixteen years later, Halford Mackinder and his Courmayeur guides skirted the massif to the north. The next visit, in 1902, was made by captain Richard Meinertzhagen who climbed to the top of Kinangop, where he built a mound two metres high and left a bottle of beer "so that the next visitor could drink to my health." The same officer made some interesting zoological discoveries

elephants, lions and large antelopes such as the shy bongo. In the dense forest dozens of waterfalls roar, including the remarkable Karuru, Chania and Gura as well as the famous Thomson's Falls.

Thanks to the abundant rains all year round many of the longest and most plentiful rivers in Kenya branch out from the Aberdares. On high, at nearly 3,500 metres, the woods give way to mountain meadows and the contorted shapes of the lobelia and groundsel.

Even higher, around the summits, rise pinnacles and spikes of

(including the eastern subspecies of the bongo and the giant warthog known by the Kikuyu as *numira*), and was involved in ferocious reprisals against some villages where white settlers had been assassinated. "It was one of my most unpleasant duties... every man and woman in the village was killed with a bullet or a bayonet thrust... we burned all the huts and razed the banana plantations to the ground" wrote Meinertzhagen in his own *Kenya Diary 1902-1906* which contains the account of his ascent to the Kinangop peak.

111 A few dozen kilometres west of the Park boundary, Lake Naivasha is an excellent place to see hippos.
Photograph by David Keith Jones/ Images of Africa Photobank

Easily reached from Nairobi, at the centre of the region of Kenya with most farms and British colonial settlements, the Aberdares very soon became popular with nature-lovers. In the Fifties, however, the clashes and massacres returned. The dense forests of these mountains provided refuge between 1952 and 1956 to the Mau Mau guerillas, the Kikuyu fighting for the independence of Kenya.

The guerilla raids spread panic among the white farmers of the plateau below. Far more violent were the British reprisals. Crack army troops burned, shot and destroyed without mercy. From an aeroplane flying over the Aberdares you can still see the craters made by the bombs dropped on the Mau Mau from the Lincolns and Meteors of the Royal Air Force.

With peace and the independence of Kenya, the extraordinary expertise in the forest of the former Mau Mau fighters was put to good use by Bill Woodley, the first chief-warden of the Park which at the time embraced both the Aberdares and Mount Kenya; he enrolled the Kikuyu guerillas as rangers.

With poaching under control the Aberdares once more became one of the most popular destinations in Africa for nature-lovers.

The luxurious lodges on the eastern side of the range, Treetops and the Ark in particular, are visited by people from all over the world.

For those wanting to spend less, in the rudimentary refuge huts and numerous campsites you will be surrounded by a splendid nature less crowded than Masai Mara or Amboseli.

The paths are short and very lovely, the treks on the Aberdares being a splendid introduction to trekking on the African mountains and accessible to all. For many hikers the climbs to the Oldoinyo Lesatima, Kinangop and the other peaks are a preparation ground for Mount Kenya.

112 top Some of the most famous hunting lodges in Africa are in the thick Aberdares forests. The picture shows an aerial view of Treetops.

112 bottom An aerial view of The Ark, a hunting lodge immersed in the thick Saliente forests.

112-113 This picture shows Treetops, an unusual construction overlooking a large watering hole used by wild animals.

113 bottom left A herd of elephants slowly approaches the buildings of The Ark without any fear.

113 bottom right An elegant female bushbuck, one of the most graceful African antelopes, appears suddenly in a clearing in the Aberdares.
Photographs by David Keith Jones/ Images of Africa Photobank

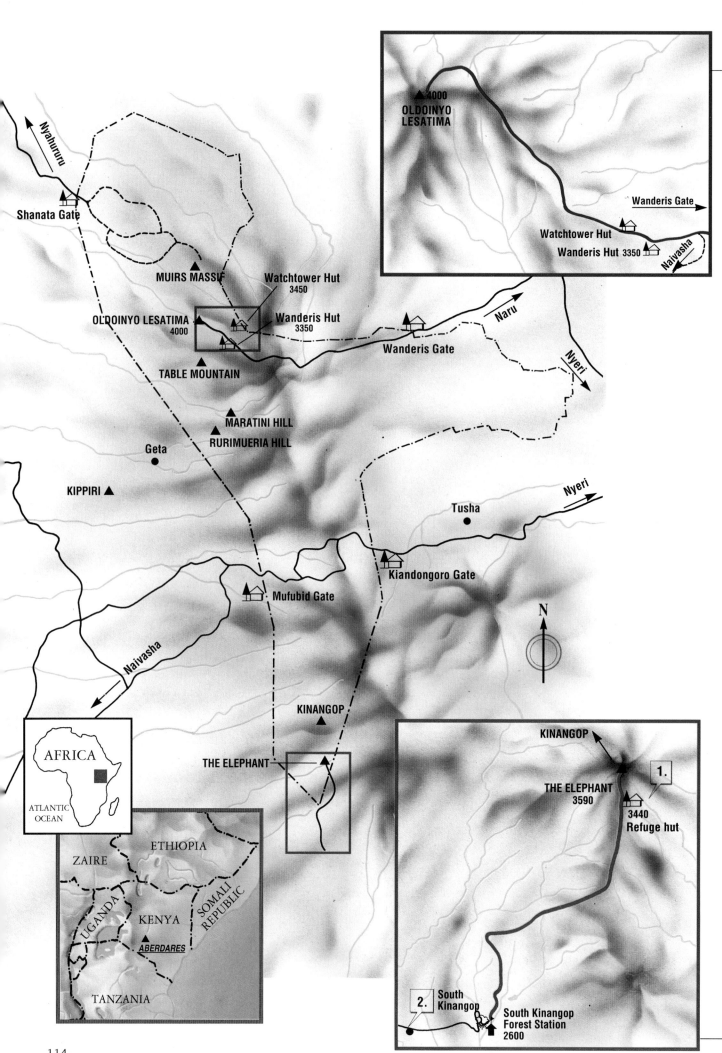

OLDOINYO LESATIMA
▲4000

Wanderis Gate →

Watchtower Hut

Wanderis Hut 3350

Naivasha ←

Nyahururu ↑

Shanata Gate

MUIRS MASSIF ▲

Watchtower Hut
3450

OL'DOINYO LESATIMA
4000 ▲

Wanderis Hut
3350

Naru →

Wanderis Gate

Nyeri →

TABLE MOUNTAIN ▲

MARATINI HILL ▲

RURIMUERIA HILL

Geta ●

KIPPIRI ▲

Tusha ●

Nyeri →

Kiandongoro Gate

Mufubid Gate

Naivasha

N

KINANGOP ▲

THE ELEPHANT

AFRICA

ATLANTIC
OCEAN

ETHIOPIA

ZAIRE

UGANDA   KENYA   SOMALI REPUBLIC

ABERDARES

TANZANIA

KINANGOP →

THE ELEPHANT
3590

1.

3440
Refuge hut

2. South Kinangop

South Kinangop
Forest Station
2600

Duration: two one/two-day excursions.
Elevation: from 2,600 to 4,000 metres.
Period: all year round, with a few problems in the small (October-November) and great rains (end March-June). The Aberdares are quite rainy at all times of the year.

Red tape: no visa is required for Kenya. Entry to the Park is by payment but there is no need to make an advance booking.
Degree of difficulty: none. Physical challenge: average
Equipment: normal gear for day excursions. Leggings are useful in the swampy parts of the path.

4 day trek that starts from Kararuru Falls and ends at the Wanderis Gate.
In case of trouble: the numerous trails in the forest permit a fairly quick evacuation of any injured persons.
Maps: the Survey of Kenya publishes a 1:50,000 map of the

A tent, sleeping bag and mattress are needed for a night at the Elephant hut. The Watchtower Hut is in reasonable condition.
Access routes: a hundred kilometres or so north of Nairobi, there are various routes to the Aberdares Park. For the paths of the eastern side of the mountain the best base is the town of Nyeri, reached from the capital via Thika and Karatina, and from where you proceed towards the Wandare and Kiandongoro gates.
Those in the south of the Park start from South Kinangop (or Njabini) reached from the Nairobi-Naivasha road.
Guides and porters: all hikers must be accompanied by an armed ranger. The short and easy excursions described here require no porters.
Detours and peaks: both the treks described lead to peaks. Other paths climb to the Kinangop (3,906 metres) and Rurimueria Hill (3,886 metres). The Park can be crossed from north to south in a

Aberdare National Park.
Alternatively there are the *Ndaragwa, Kipipiri* and *Kinangop* sheets.
Guidebooks: itineraries on the Aberdares are described in *Trekking in East Africa* by David Else (Lonely Planet, 1993), *Mountain Walking in Africa 1 - Kenya* by David Else (Robertson McCarta, 1990) and in *Backpacker's Africa - East and Southern* by Hilary Bradt (Bradt-Hunter, 1989).
For further reading: there is an interesting chapter on the Aberdares in *Snowcaps on the Equator* by Iain Allen, Gordon Boy and Clive Ward (The Bodley Head, 1989).

115 top left
The helichrysum in bloom colour the high altitude steppe of the Aberdares. This is the Oldoinyo Lesatima ridge at about 3,500 metres above sea level.

115 bottom left
Between 2,000 and 2,500 metres, the slopes of the massif are covered with a thick bamboo forest.
Photographs by David Keith Jones/ Images of Africa Photobank

115 right
The equatorial forest covering part of the central Aberdares is similar to that of mountains such as Mount Kenya and Kilimanjaro.
Photograph by Carla Signorini Jones/Images of Africa Photobank

FROM THE WANDERIS HUT TO OLDOINYO LESATIMA

ONE-DAY TREK
distance climbed: 400-650 metres
time: 4-6 hours

Short and with no particular difficulties, this trek to the highest peak of the Aberdares from the Nyeri and Naro Moru side is the most popular of the whole chain.
From Nyeri go to the Park offices at Mweiga from where another 18 kilometres lead to the Wanderis Gate. Continue along the road for another 12 kilometres to a fork in the road. Bear right and in one kilometre you will come to the Wanderis Hut (3,350 metres); another 2 kilometres lead to the Watchtower Hut (3,450 metres), the best place for the night in the area. The last stretch of the trail may be inaccessible to vehicles after heavy rains. Continue along the trail which ends after another two kilometres on a broad ridge (3,600 metres). A path proceeds along the ridge, descending into a large pass and starts to climb again at the foot of a band of grey rocks. Once at the summit plateau, cross it to the mound on the peak (4,000 metres). It takes 2 hours 30 minutes from the end of the trail, 3 hours 30 minutes from the Watchtower Hut and 4 hours from the Wanderis Hut. The descent is of course faster.

116 top A trekker on the wide ridge leading to the top of Oldoinyo Lesatima (4,000 metres), the highest peak in the Aberdares.
Photograph by Stefano Ardito

116 centre Occasional scenic spots on the trail climbing to the Wanderis Hut show the remarkable
wild forests that cover the central Aberdares.
Photograph by Stefano Ardito

116 bottom The path that descends from the summital crest of The Elephant to the refuge hut is immersed in thick vegetation.
Photograph by Stefano Ardito

SECOND DAY

from the hut
to the peak and South Kinangop
distance climbed: 150 metres
distance descended: 1,000 metres
time: 5-6 hours

From the refuge hut follow the trail that leads to the Elephant summit, along which you will find several peaks. The highest is the second from the left (3,590 metres) reached in half an hour after having passed a saddle. From the highest point a small fairly obvious path leads to the other peaks on the mountain. Those with an extra day can (only with a guide and in good weather) also reach the Kinangop peak which takes approximately 6 hours return from the refuge hut.
The descent to South Kinangop is via the same way as the ascent.

FROM SOUTH KINANGOP TO THE ELEPHANT

FIRST DAY

from South Kinangop
to the refuge hut
distance climbed: 850 metres
time: 5 hours 30 minutes

At the southernmost tip of the chain, the Elephant peak offers a rather long trek of extreme environmental interest, with a succession of coniferous woods, tropical forest and bamboo. Some parts of the trek are rather muddy. It can be done in one day but it is far better to camp for the night at the abandoned refuge hut before the top so as to enjoy the views with the clear morning sky. From South Kinangop in 3 kilometres you will come to the forest station of the

same name (2,600 metres). From here proceed on foot along a wide forest trail (part of this can be covered with a 4x4 vehicle) to and along a crest. Once past a landslide proceed in zigzags for a stretch. A not always clearly visible path climbs in the bamboo forest to a grassy hill and then the refuge hut (3,440 metres) within sight of the four mountain peaks.

117 left
A herd of buffalo graze in a clearing in the thick Aberdares forests. The sudden appearance of these
animals can be very dangerous for the trekker.
Photograph by David Keith Jones/ Images of Africa Photobank

117 top right
Much of the path that climbs from South Kinangop to the Elephant passes through the bamboo forest.
Photograph by David Keith Jones/ Images of Africa Photobank

117 bottom right
The distant peak of Mount Kenya behind the Treetops lake, one of the most popular lodges in the Aberdares.
Photograph by David Keith Jones/ Images of Africa Photobank

MOUNT KENYA

In search of the "African Matterhorn"

Great sheets of reddish volcanic rock, rough to the touch. Sheer rock faces furrowed by vertical crevices, masses poised in equilibrium, backdrops highlighted by the morning light. You climb zigzag up, in search of the least problematical passages. High up an easy canal leads to the Nelion peak, then a snowcovered saddle - the Gate of Mists - precedes the heaped blocks of the Batian peak. A few metres and there is the highest point, the "African Matterhorn", 5,199 metres above sea level. From the Batian peak the gaze sweeps over the Teleki and Mackinder valleys, already invaded by the first clouds. To the west the green crests of the Aberdares, densely blanketed with forest, dominate the fertile Kikuyu plateau. Far away, southwards, floating on a sea of clouds is the icy peak of Kilimanjaro. There is no need to climb the highest peaks just to see. From the 4,985 metres of the Lenana Peak, reached every year by thousands of trekkers, one can admire the spectacle of sunrise over the Nelion rocks. Fifty years ago Felice Benuzzi described them as "shining a yellow like that of the houses of old Rome in autumn, before the sunset turns them vermillion". Lower down, in the mists at 4,000 metres, you walk long through senecious groundsel and lobelia, the fairy tale, colossal succulents present on all the African mountains. Eagles, vultures and the splendid giant Mackinder owl often appear in the sky. Traces in the mud and excrement may betray the passage of several buffaloes and a leopard. Even farther down, around three thousand metres, the forest of Mount Kenya displays an enchantment made of giant, swaying heathers, of podocarps and macaranga with the highest of trunks, so loved by the howling colobus monkeys. From the fertile plain below, the mountain looks like a beautiful, regular pyramid. This vision has moved travellers and mountaineers alike. And much earlier made Mount Kenya the Olympus of the nearby populations.

"Mogai, the father of the universe, created Kere-Nyaga, the dazzling mountain, as a place of rest and sign of his miracles for men. When he created Kikuyu, the progenitor of the race, he took him to the summit and showed him the beauties of the country. "Should he ever be in need - he was told - he was to raise his hands to the mountain. And he, the Lord, would come to his aid." This is the genesis of the world according to the Kikuyu, the farming and herding people of the great plateaux of Kenya, as told by Jomo Kenyatta, the leader of the movement for independence and in 1961 the country's first head of State. The title of his autobiography *Facing Mount Kenya* illustrates more than many words the importance of this peak for the local people. Until the beginning of the century the Masai populated the plateau between Mount Kenya and the Aberdares. Amidst the rocks they worshipped Ngai (or Eng-ai), the goddess who dispenses rain and fine weather. For them the mountain was Ol-Donyo-Eibor, the "white mountain". For the Meru, who live north-east of the massif, all human races originated up there. For the Samburu the mountain is Lorgenai, the "black stone" - and from their position the mountain does appear mainly rocky. It was the Kikuyu name, however, which gave the present name to the mountain and the country - Kere-Nyaga. Then Ke-e-nya-a, later to become Kenya. In 1848 the peak saw the first caravans of European explorers pass. The first was the Swiss reverend Johann Rebmann, followed by his colleague and fellow-countryman Ludwig Krapf.

Joseph Thomson a Scottish naturalist, saw and described in 1885 a "shining peak twinkling with the superb beauty of a diamond". Two years later, the Hungarian count Samuel Teleki climbed up to 4,700 metres. In 1893 the Englishman J.W. Gregory discovered that the mountain is what remains of an ancient volcano. In 1899 the Scotsman Halford Mackinder and the guides of Courmayeur Cesare Ollier and Giuseppe Brocherel (who became "Swiss guides" for the British authors) used a new railway route from the port of Mombasa to the plain where Nairobi was being built. On foot, in twenty days, they arrived to the base of the mountain. On 20 August the caravan entered the high altitude forest. On 12-13 September the expertise and intuition of the Mont Blanc guides enabled the group to reach the 5,199 metres of the summit. The way was difficult, with passages up to 4th degree on rock and three hours of work with an ice axe to make steps in the short but very hard slope named at the time the "Diamond Glacier". At the foot of the mountain, the Masai clans disturbed the expedition, killing a porter. Mackinder, as a mark of respect for this warfaring people ("it was right that a memory of those noble savages should remain in history" - he was to write) used some of their chiefs' names for the peaks known today as Batian, Nelion, Lenana and Sendeyo. In 1929 the plateau at the foot of Mount Kenya was already home to the tidy succession of farms described by Karen Blixen in her *Out of Africa*. Eric Shipton, later known for his great Himalayan expeditions, tells of "how it may seem ridiculous... to arrive on a African farm with an ice axe, climbing boots and dozens of yards of rope". Together with Percy Wyn Harris, the young Eric attempted Batian from the north-east, then reached it climbing the Nelion peak. The following year, with Bill Tilman, Shipton conquered the difficult west ridge of the highest peak. These ascents transported mountaineering into a sports dimension in Africa too. There is, however, another important page in history to be told. Nanyuki, in 1942, hosted a thousand or so Italian prisoners. One of these, Felice Benuzzi, suddenly saw a "silvery, sharp, [mountain] enveloped in cloud" surrounded by "glaciers seemingly suspended in nothing, unreal". Hope sprang forth. In the following months,

Benuzzi brought Giovanni Balletto and Vincenzo Barsotti into his adventure. Pieces of the hemp nets from the camp beds were used to plaid ropes; iron scraps became rudimentary ice axes and crampons. A little food was set aside from the meagre portions. The only information they had on Mount Kenya was a picture of it on the label of a tin of meat. On 24 January 1943, the three Italians escaped from Camp 354; they plunged into the forest and climbed far from the paths, experiencing the odd dangerous encounter with elephants and rhinoceros. On 4 February Benuzzi and Balletto attacked the west ridge of the Batian peak, the most difficult route in the worst season. They climbed a good stretch of it, redescending in the storm. Two days later they climbed the easy Lenana Peak, where they left a homemade tricolour flag. They then dragged themselves down to the valley and handed themselves back to the English. In admiration the commander of Camp 354 reduced the days of punishment from 28 to 7. Once peace had come, Benuzzi's book *(No Picnic on Mount Kenya)* became a best seller of mountain literature. Today, the silent valleys faced by Mackinder, Shipton and the three Italian prisoners are crowded with more than 15,000 hikers every year. Comfortable refuge huts have been built all over; the Lenana Peak where Benuzzi and friends savoured their "victory over the sluggish prison routine" is trodden by dozens of trekkers every day. Climbing to the Batian and Nelion peaks, you will come across nails, ropes, traces of previous passages every few metres. But the nature still exists. Of the many Kenyan parks that protecting the mountain is the highest, the only one that can be explored solely on foot, the hardest to guard because of the dense forest. The rhinoceros have disappeared as a result of the relentless hunting but the elephants, buffaloes and leopards are there, as well as the small, shy antelopes of the forest such as the duiker and the bushbuck. Among the treks to the three great mountains of Africa, the climb to Kilimanjaro is a personal challenge in defiance of the altitude, that to Ruwenzori is a great adventure in mud and wilderness. The trek to Mount Kenya is easier to organize, the

most spectacular, that with the richest scenery. It is also the most varied as you can choose between the three paths climbing towards the heart of the massif. An encounter with buffaloes, senecious groundsel and the legends of the Masai will remind you that you are in the heart of black Africa.

120 Like the other great mountains in Africa, Mount Kenya is marked by the presence of senecious groundsel. Those in the picture grow not far from the Teleki Lodge, at the foot of the northern side of the highest peaks.

121 top Zebras are often seen on the plateaux around Mount Kenya and in the Meru National Park, to the north-east of the range.

121 bottom Situated slightly north of Nairobi, Mount Kenya is inhabited by the most typical species of eastern African fauna. Different animals such as the Somali giraffe appear just a little farther north, in the barren savannah past Isiolo. Photographs by Stefano Ardito

USEFUL INFORMATION

Duration: 6-7 days but treks lasting from 2-3 days to two weeks are possible on this mountain.

Elevation: from 2,600 (or 3,350) to 4,985 or 5,199 metres.

Period: For the trekker the best period coincides with the two dry seasons in Kenya - from December to March and from the end of June to September. Matters are more complicated for the mountaineer who must take into consideration the mountain's position on the Equator. In our summer it is free from snow on the north side and the rock routes on this side and the icy ones exposed southwards are in the right conditions. In the austral summer (July-August) the situation is the reverse. The climbing route is feasible from December to March.

Red tape: no visa is required for Kenya. The entrance to the Park is open to all with no need for reservations and just payment of 300 shillings per day per person.

Degree of diffilculty: no technical problems. The climb to the Lenana Peak, made at dawn, requires care on the easy Lewis Glacier slopes. Particularly laborious are the peat bogs of "Vertical bog" on the descent via the Naro Moru route.

Physical challenge: average. The altitude is rather high but the trek is decidedly less tiring than the climb on Kilimanjaro.

Equipment: normal trekking gear plus a pair of leggings (useful in the swampy parts) and ski sticks. Along the Naro Moru, Sirimon and Chogoria routes you always sleep in refuge huts: a tent may be useful should the Teleki Lodge or the Austrian Hut be crowded. A sleeping bag is needed. For the climb to the highest peaks full rock climbing gear with rope, harness, helmet, nails, snaplinks, and chocks is required. An ice axe and crampons are essential for the short but troublesome crossing from the Nelion to Batian peaks.

Access routes: Naro Moru and Nanyuki are approximately 150 kilometres from each other and are reached in about three hours from Nairobi. There are frequent bus and air connections.

Guides and porters: the lodges at the base of the mountain and, in particular, the Naro Moru River Lodge and Bantu Lodge (or Mountain Rock Lodge) can organize the trek providing board, equipment, porters and guides. The most economical solution is to hire porters personally in the village of Naro Moru or even take all the necessary in your rucksack. Park rules forbid hiking alone for safety reasons.

HAUSBERG VALLEY

TELEKI VALLE

Naro Moru Gate 7 Km

Naro Moru Route

6. 3050 Met Station

Detours and peaks: Lenana (4,985 metres) is a sensational scenic spot and is reached by most trekkers visiting the park. The climb to the Nelion (5,188 metres) and the Batian (5,199 metres) peaks described here is a demanding climb. Other peaks such as the Terere and Sendeyo can be reached without difficulty.

In case of trouble: the rangers of Mount Kenya National Park can intervene should there be an accident. They can be called at the Teleki Valley control post (just above

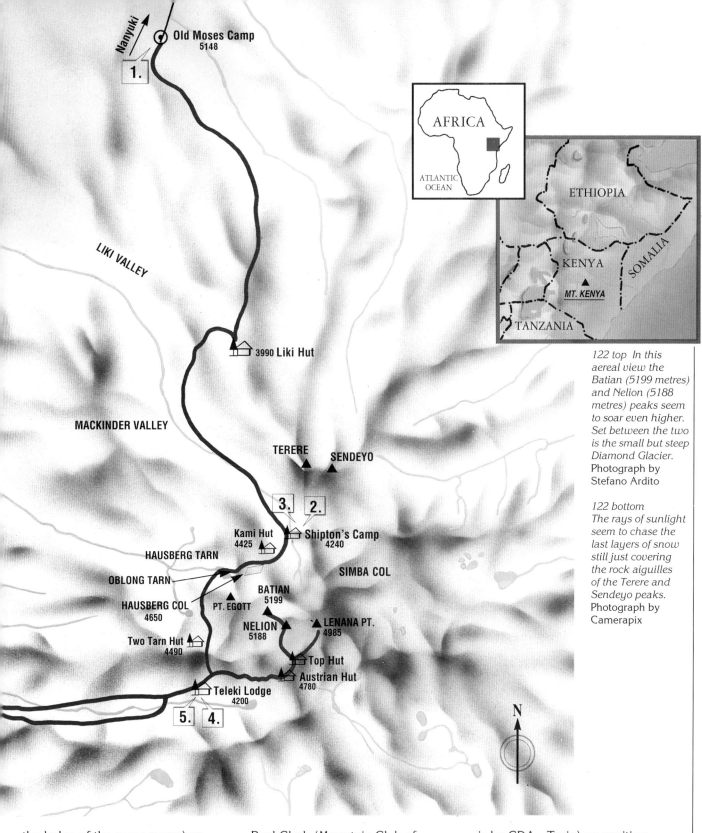

Nanyuki

Old Moses Camp
5148

1.

LIKI VALLEY

3990 Liki Hut

MACKINDER VALLEY

TERERE   SENDEYO

3. 2.

Kami Hut
4425   Shipton's Camp
4240

HAUSBERG TARN

OBLONG TARN

SIMBA COL

HAUSBERG COL
4650   PT. EGOTT

BATIAN
5199

NELION
5188   LENANA PT.
4985

Two Tarn Hut
4490

Top Hut

Austrian Hut
4780

Teleki Lodge
4200

5. 4.

N

AFRICA

ATLANTIC
OCEAN

ETHIOPIA

KENYA   SOMALIA

MT. KENYA

TANZANIA

122 top In this
aereal view the
Batian (5199 metres)
and Nelion (5188
metres) peaks seem
to soar even higher.
Set between the two
is the small but steep
Diamond Glacier.
Photograph by
Stefano Ardito

122 bottom
The rays of sunlight
seem to chase the
last layers of snow
still just covering
the rock aiguilles
of the Terere and
Sendeyo peaks.
Photograph by
Camerapix

the lodge of the same name) or by contacting the refuge huts on the mountain.
Maps: it is easy to find the *Mount Kenya* map by Andrew Wielochowski and Mark Savage in Nairobi.
Guidebooks: treks on Mount Kenya are described in numerous publications including *Guide to Mount Kenya and Kilimanjaro* by Iain Allen (Mountain Club of Kenya, 1982), the *East Africa International Mountain Guide* by Andrew Wielochowski (West Col, 1986), *The Mountains of Kenya* by

Paul Clark (Mountain Club of Kenya). The treks on the mountain are described in detail in *Mountain Walking in Africa 1 - Kenya* by David Else (Robertson McCarta, 1990) and in *Backpacker's Africa - East and Southern* by Hilary Bradt (Bradt-Hunter 1989).
For further reading: before leaving you can read the bulky *Sui ghiacciai dell'Africa* by Mario Fantin (Cappelli, 1968). In the rucksack you can find room for *No Picnic on Mount Kenya* by Felice Benuzzi (the current edition

is by CDA - Turin) an exciting account of the 1943 Italian feat. Also of interest are *Snowcaps on the Equator* by G. Boy, I. Allan and C. Ward (The Bodley Head, 1988), *Mount Kenya* by John Reader (Elm Tree Books, 1989) and *The first Ascent of Mount Kenya* by H.J. Mackinder (Hurst & Company, 1990). For naturalists we recommend *National Parks of* East Africa by J.G. Williams (Collins, 1981) or *Kenya and Tanzania* by H. and W. Hagen (Zanichelli, 1993).

124 top The first section of the Sirimon route crosses the desolate and spectacular savannah between Old Moses Camp and the Liki Hut. Visible in the background are the Terere, Sendeyo and - farther right - Nelion and Batian peaks.

*124 centre
A trekker and his Kikuyu guide hike through groundsel and mist in Mackinder Valley, at about 4,000 metres above sea level.*

*124 bottom
At 4,100 metres the path that climbs to Shipton's Camp passes beside the small Mackinder's Caves; these sheltered the first mountaineers to visit the mountain.*

FIRST DAY

*from Nanyuki to the Old Moses Camp
distance climbed: 700 metres
time: 3 hours 30 minutes*

A 9-kilometre trail separates the asphalt Nairobi-Nanyuki-Isiolo road from the Sirimon Gate (2,650 metres) of Mount Kenya National Park. From here a trail usually open to vehicles proceeds across a magnificent forest to the Judmeier Camp clearing and the nearby Old Moses Camp (3,350 metres), a large refuge hut already in the world of heather and rocks. To acclimatize to the altitude and admire the vegetation without haste this part should be covered on foot: it takes half a day and is an excellent approach to the mountain.

SECOND DAY

*from the Old Moses camp
to Shipton's camp
distance climbed: 1,090 metres
distance descended: 200 metres
time: 7 hours*

A long and rather tiring day leading to the base of the northern slopes of the Nelion and Batian peaks.
The poor conditions of the Liki Hut make it definitely advisable to proceed to the comfortable Shipton's Camp. Walk along the broad, grassy ridge overlooking the Old Moses Camp; it is a fairly well marked path from which the Nelion and Batian are a breathtaking sight. Close to a large isolated mass go sharp right, cross a ridge and descend crossways to the badly kept Liki Hut (3,990 metres). Then climb and pass over a ridge to enter on a steep descent the spectacular Mackinder Valley, through rocks and groundsel.
After following a rocky strip where various species of birds of prey nest, you will come to Shipton's Camp (4,240 metres) dominated by the northern slope of the Batian and Nelion peaks. The "low path" crosses towards Mackinder Valley avoiding the Liki Hut saving a climb of 200 metres and 1 hour 30 minutes' march.

124-125 The Nelion and Batian peaks appear in all their grandeur before Teleki Lodge (4,200 metres), the most popular hut on Mount Kenya.

125 bottom left A trekker stops amid the groundsel of the upper Mackinder Valley, within sight of the Terere and Sendeyo peaks.

125 bottom right The highest peaks of Mount Kenya serve as a backdrop to the comfortable Shipton's Camp (4,240 metres). The Nelion and

Batian massif is at the centre, to the right is the yellowish Peter's Point, to the left Lenana Peak. **Photographs by Stefano Ardito**

125

THIRD DAY
around Shipton's Camp
distance climbed and descended:
as desired
time: as desired

After quickly reaching 4,000 metres, it is most certainly worth dedicating a day to rest and acclimatization within sight of the magnificent Batian and Nelion faces. The rocky ridges dominating the refuge hut from the north-east are an obvious choice for a hike of a couple of hours. Trained trekkers with climbing experience can devote their attention to the graceful Terere and Sendeyo peaks. From Shipton's Camp you can also climb to the top of Lenana in 3-4 hours along the steep path passing Simba Col.

FOURTH DAY
from Shipton's Camp to Teleki Lodge
distance climbed: 550 metres
distance descended: 660 metres
time: 4 hours

A magnificent day on which you skirt the main peaks to the east, passing the small refuge huts of Kami and Two Tarn. There is a splendid view of the rocky towers and suspended glaciers of the west face of the Batian, as well as of the romantic lakes (Oblong Tarn and Hausberg Tarn) surrounded by groundsel and where Benuzzi, Barsotti and Balletto camped in 1943. The path rises quickly to the Kami Hut (4,425 metres) and continues along a steep, awkward, stony slope to the Hausberg Col (4,650 metres) from where it descends steeply to the lakes. A less tiring climb and a stretch across the mountain along broad rocky ledges lead to the small Two Tarn Hut (4,490 metres), another splendid viewpoint over the Batian serracs. A horizontal stretch and a stony descent will take you to the spacious Teleki Lodge building (4,200 metres), the most popular refuge hut on the mountain. At sunset the view of the Nelion and Batian peaks with the remarkable and icy Diamond Couloir between them is magnificent.

FIFTH DAY

*from Teleki Lodge
to the Lenana Peak and back
distance climbed: 780 metres
distance descended: 780 metres
time: 5 hours*

After leaving Teleki Lodge the path
heads for a while almost on the flat
eastwards at the foot of the spectacular
southern Nelion and Batian faces.
It then climbs at length along tiring
screes (often compared to those of
Gillman's Point on Mount Kibo, but in
actual fact far more kindly) to a short
distance before the broad ridge that
descends to the south from the Lenana
Peak. A last stretch slightly downwards
leads to the Austrian Hut (4,780
metres), the base for those wishing
to attempt the ascent to the Nelion and
Batian summits. Nearby are the small

and badly kept Top Hut and an icy
lake that can be used for water
supplies. Start off again along the
broad gravely ridge, leaving it farther
on to the left for the easy snowfields
marking the edge of the Lewis Glacier.
A last steeper stretch will take you to
the Lenana Peak (4,985 metres), the
"roof" of the mountain for the hiker
and offering an extraordinary view over
the eastern face of the Nelion, the
surrounding valleys and the distant
Kilimanjaro. From Mackinder Valley
it takes three hours: you usually leave
in the darkness to arrive to the summit
at dawn. The descent is easily
completed in two hours.

128-129 In the vicinity of the Austrian Hut, the eyes sweep over the wide Lewis Glacier, the green waters of Lewis Tarn and the John Sharp Point. Photograph by David Keith Jones/ Images of Africa Photobank

128 bottom left Just above Teleki Lodge, the path that climbs to the Austrian Hut passes the base of the spectacular northern faces of the Nelion and Batian, furrowed by the narrow band of ice called Diamond's Couloir. Photograph by Cl. Jaccoux/Agence Freestyle

128 bottom right A girl is watching the lobelia that grows at the foot of the Kenya massif. Photograph by Stefano Ardito

the southern ridge and the Baillie camp (5,000 metres). Cross over the ridge to reach and climb the graceful De Graaf dihedron (IV+, the loveliest and most flowing passage on the route) beyond which you cross again to the right with another IV stretch. An easier canal-chimney leads to the Nelion summit (5,188 metres); from here a not easy crossing (III+ passages) requiring the use of an ice axe and crampons will lead you to the Batian peak (5,199 metres). The descent from the Nelion involves a dozen or so descents with double ropes. Those arriving late can spend the night at the small Howell camp, on the very top of the Nelion summit.

SIXTH DAY
from Teleki Lodge
to the Met Station and Naro Moru
distance climbed: 80 metres
distance descended: 1,189 metres
time: 5 hours

Long but without difficulty, the last day of the trek leads back to the magical world of the forest and the valley bottom. Start on the orographical right of the wide Teleki Valley, then cross the river and proceed at length across the mountain on the opposite side through the magnificent groundsel and lobelia. There are two paths in this part: the lower one is usually muddier. The path reaches the rocky ridge closing the valley, continuing in zigzags along various points, then descends abruptly through increasingly damp meadows. Once across the peat bogs known as "Vertical Bog" you will enter the heather forest. A good path reaches the Met Station (3,050 metres) connected by a 7 kilometres dirt track to the Naro Moru gate. On foot this part takes another 2 hours. A further 18 kilometres will take you back to Naro Moru.

VARIATION TO THE FIFTH DAY
The ascent to the Nelion and Batian peaks from the Austrian Hut
distance climbed and descended:
420 metres
time: 8-12 hours

The normal ascent route to the highest peaks of Mount Kenya is a demanding mountaineering one with difficulties up to IV+ in the ascent to the Nelion and mixed stretches in the crossing to the Batian. From the Austrian Hut cross the not difficult Lewis Glacier from where a tiring scree leads to the point of attack. Climb up easy crevices, then cross right to the base of the Mackinder chimney where strands of the 1899 rope remain.
A hard crevice (One o'Clock Gully, IV+ passage) and a broad dihedron lead to the easy rocks that precede

129 top
The east face of the Nelion is on the normal route up to both of the highest peaks. The start is in the large gravel hollow on the left, the route then climbs diagonally to the right.
Photograph by Marco Majrani

129 centre
A diagonal rock is the last difficulty before the easy channel that leads to the Nelion peak.
Photograph by Stefano Ardito

129 bottom Lenana Peak overlooks the Austrian Hut.
Photograph by Stefano Ardito

KILIMANJARO: ON THE ROOF OF AFRICA

Two routes to the 5,895 metres
of Uhuru Peak

When the sky clears behind Mawenzi the worst has passed. Suddenly, as always in the Tropics, the light of dawn rises from the Indian Ocean and the Tsavo hills giving form to the bizarre rocky pinnacles dedicated to Meyer, Purtscheller and Klute. Lower down, on the plain, the light announcing the coming day engulfs the lights of Moshi, faithful companions of the hours spent groping in the dark on the interminable gravels of Mount Kibo. A fairytale world seems within grasp. Left, the steps of the Rebmann glacier climb evenly to the crater. On the edge of the great caldera rise needles and spikes of reddish lava, separated by screes and snowfields. The paunchy Bismarck Towers are skirted on an easy slope. Then a broad ridge of snow furrowed by kindly crevices leads to the highest summit, Uhuru Peak, "freedom" in Swahili. In just a kilometre of ridge lies a century of Africa's history. "As wide as all the world, great, high, and incredibly white in the sun,". Thus, in 1938, Ernest Hemingway described the "square top" of the volcano in his *Snows of Kilimanjaro* (Bantam Books, 1976). The writer from Chicago never climbed to the top. He did admire it at length from the base, from Loitokitok, on the border between Kenya and Tanganyika, where for years he was an honorary ranger. Walking on the edge of the crater in the light of dawn you can at last appreciate an overused quotation. You move on a platform of deep snow, with no other mountains in sight, navigating on a ghost ship suspended on the sea of clouds that conceals the savannah. Of the day leading to the summit, the first part is one of brutal fatigue. Leaving the Kibo refuge hut between midnight and 1 a.m. you climb up a reasonable path to the Hans Meyer Cave and proceed along menacing screes to Gillman's Point, 5,685 metres above sea-level. The second part, on the

edge of the crater, is less tiring but far more exciting. At 5,895 metres, on the Uhuru Peak, is a little heap of stones, flags faded by sun and wind and a bronze plaque. Here, on 9 December 1961, the torch of independence of the new Tanganyika was lit; three years later the country became Tanzania. "We would like this light to shine beyond the borders, bringing hope, love and dignity." These are the words engraved in bronze, the

130 Shortly before the Horombo Hut, the path up to the top of Mount Kibo passes through lovely scenery marked by lobelia and groundsel.

131 A stream runs through the splendid rain forest that covers the lower part of the mountain, not far from the Marangu Path. Photographs by Marco Majrani

words of Julius Nyerere, the country's first President. Of the mountains of Africa, Kilimanjaro is the highest, the least humid, that closest to the sea. Anything but secret, it is nothing like the fabulous Ruwenzori enveloped in clouds and perpetual mist. Before this peak Europe has experienced a curious amnesia. Ptolemy had written of a "great snow-covered mountain". During our Middle Ages similar words could be found in the writings of various Chinese historians. In 1519 the Spaniard Fernandes de Enciso told of the "Olympus of Ethiopia, west of Mombasa, that is very high, in a land rich in gold and wild animals". The first European to see it, on 11 May 1848, was the Swiss missionary

Johann Rebmann. "I saw something white at the top of the Chagga village mountain. My guides did not know the name but they used the word cold. It was snow." It seemed a logical observation and it is obvious to suppose that a Swiss man - albeit at the Equator - should know about snow. In London, however, the famous geographer William D. Cooley defined Rebmann's report as "an absurd, immaginary, unproven vision." The dispute continued for years. A German nobleman, Karl Kaus von Decken, ended all the arguments raised by Rebmann when, in 1861, he made the first attempt at the peak. He stopped before reaching 3,000 metres but brought the first accurate description of the mountain back to Europe.

132-133 By making a night departure from the Kibo or Barafu Huts trekkers can reach the Uhuru Peak (5,895 metres), *the highest point in Africa, with the magic light of dawn.* Photograph by Stefano Ardito

He told of the forest at the base and the desert plain separating Mount Kibo from the rocks of Mawenzi, the second highest peak on the range. In the meantime other Germans were laying the foundations for an empire in Africa.

In 1886, according to tradition, Queen Victoria herself decided to give Kilimanjaro to her nephew, the future Kaiser William II. "I am astonished that some of our most sober men should want to annex a mountain with an unpronounceable name in the vicinity of Zanzibar" the British Prime Minister William Gladstone cried at a government meeting on 14 December 1884. But it was destiny that Kilimanjaro be linked with Germany. In 1887 Hans Meyer, a professor and topographer from Liepzig, led a fresh series of attempts at the peak. He reached it on 6 October 1889 together with Ludwig Purtscheller, a famous mountaineer from Salzburg. "At half past ten I set foot on the central peak. With a triple hurrah I planted a small German flag... I called the Kibo summit, the highest point of German and African land, Kaiser Wilhelm Spitze" he wrote in his report. In 1912 Walther Furtwangler and Siegfried Konig skied all the way around the crater. In 1938, two mountaineers from Stuttgart opened the first route on the south side of Kibo, that along the spectacular Decken glacier.

Tanganyika came under the control of Great Britain in 1918 but the highest peak in Africa bore the Kaiser's name until 1961.

Today, the highest mountain in Africa has become one of the best loved destination of trekkers the world over. Groups organized by the European mountaineering clubs, Americans following in the footsteps of Hemingway and "relentless" Englishmen come overland from Europe, all take the wide path starting from Marangu.

After all, it is extremely rare for a mountain to permit an ascent to almost 6,000 metres without any technical difficulties. At first the route crosses a magnificent forest of podocarps and macarangas to reach the Mandara Hut; it proceeds amidst spectacular giant heathers to the Horombo clearing and refuge hut within sight of Mount Kibo.

Next comes the remarkable Sella desert and a - for many sleepless - night at the 4,700 metres of the Kibo Hut. The last stretch, on the steep screes that accompany the trekker towards the crater, often shatters dreams of success. The demanding climb from 5,100 to 5,700 metres has no mercy for lack of training and tenacity. Even if you do not reach the top, however, your adventure on Kilimanjaro will never be forgotten. The Marangu route is not the only one. Wilder, more spectacular and less popular, the route starting from Machame is the most preferable on the mountain. You climb through a magnificent forest towards the Shira plateau, descending into the extraordinary Barranco Valley and climbing to the summit via a gorge of stones and snow less demanding than the normal route. Harder, but again without technical demands, is the route from Shira to the peak via the Arrow Glacier Hut and the Western Breach.

For mountaineers and of average difficulty, on the other hand, are the routes via the steep, rough Heim and Decken glaciers and the mixed routes leading to the Mawenzi peaks. For mountaineers who love thrills there is Breach Wall, the dark, threatening face coated with frightening vertical streams of ice. Battered by showers of ice and stones, this route was opened in 1978 by Reinhold Messner and Konrad Renzler. The spectacle of the forest, the ice steps, the birds of prey and the high altitude vegetation will excite the best mountaineers and the meekest high altitude wayfarers alike.

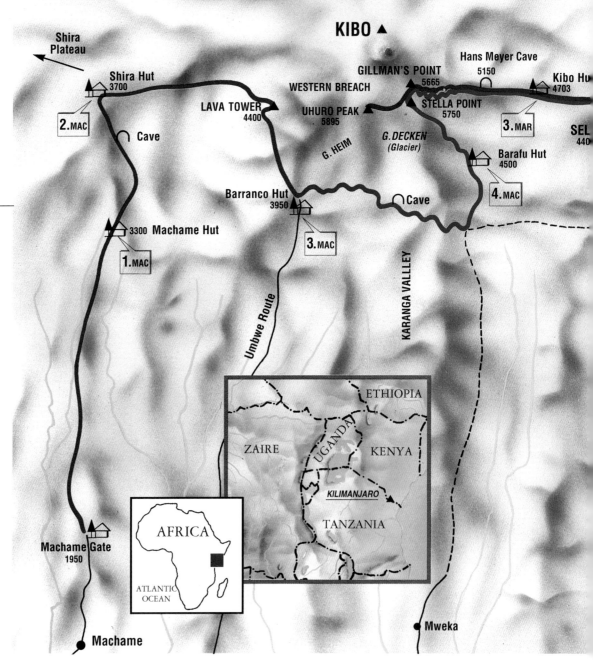

135 top *A notice beside the Marangu gate, the busiest in the Kilimanjaro National Park, indicates altitudes, distances and habitat of the refuge huts and the peak.* Fotografia di Stefano Ardito

135 bottom *It is not unusual to encounter Masai in their colourful head-dresses on the roads leading to the foot of Kilimanjaro.* Photograph by Marcello Bertinetti/ White Star Archive

KIBO ▲

Shira Plateau

Shira Hut
3700

2. MAC

Cave

LAVA TOWER
4400

WESTERN BREACH

Hans Meyer Cave
5150

GILLMAN'S POINT
5665

UHURO PEAK
5895

STELLA POINT
5750

3. MAR

Kibo Hu
4703

SEL
440

G. HEIM

G. DECKEN
(Glacier)

Barafu Hut
4500

4. MAC

Barranco Hut
3950

3. MAC

3300 Machame Hut

1. MAC

Cave

KARANGA VALLLEY

Umbwe Route

Machame Gate
1950

ETHIOPIA

ZAIRE

UGANDA

KENYA

KILIMANJARO

TANZANIA

AFRICA

ATLANTIC OCEAN

Mweka

Machame

USEFUL INFORMATION

Duration: 5 days for the Marangu route, 6 days via Machame. Adding one or two days is recommended for acclimatization but the already high costs rise.

Elevation: from 1,980 metres (Marangu route) or 1,900 metres (via Machame) to 5,895 metres.

Period: the best period coincides with the two dry seasons in Tanzania - from December to March and from the end of June to September.

Red tape: a visa is required for Tanzania. The entrance to the Park costs nearly 400 dollars and must be paid at the Marangu Gate even if you intend using a different route.

Degree of difficulty: the Marangu route presents no technical problems but the steep screes separating the 5,200 metres of Hans Meyer Cave from Gillman's Point are quite rightly known as one of the most exhausting trekker routes on any mountain in the world. Wrongly indicated as "difficult" by official literature, the Machame route may call for the use of an ice axe and crampons on the last 200 metres preceding the crater. The screes are shorter and more solid than those of the most popular route. In all cases, the high altitude requires good training and a keen lookout for symptoms of mountain sickness.

Physical challenge: very high because of the altitude and the fast climb to 5,000 metres. The ascent of Kilimanjaro is harder than a long

trek in the Himalayas where the same altitude is reached after one or two weeks' hike.

Equipment: normal trekking gear but with excellent clothing for the cold of the ascent to the top. Ski sticks are very useful both going up and down. Crampons (and perhaps an ice axe) are recommended for the Machame route. A tent is needed on the Machame route but unnecessary on the Marangu one. A sleeping bag is required everywhere. The refuge huts on the usual route are spacious and comfortable; those on the Machame route are far more rudimentary and used by the porters: trekkers camp in the vicinity.

Access routes: Marangu, at the foot of Kilimanjaro, is 23 kilometres from Moshi, 80 from Arusha and 55 from

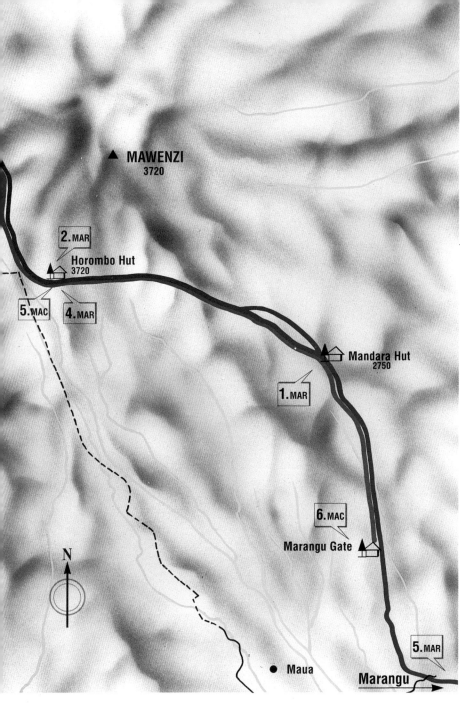

▲ MAWENZI
3720

2.MAR

Horombo Hut
3720

5.MAC   4.MAR

Mandara Hut
2750

1.MAR

N

6.MAC

Marangu Gate

5.MAR

● Maua

Marangu

Kilimanjaro International Airport,
reached via Dar-es-Salaam, Nairobi,
or on direct flights from Europe.
It can be reached by road from
Kenya on the Nairobi-Arusha
(273 kilometres) road and the
Mombasa-Voi-Moshi (277
kilometres) road. From Marangu
the asphalt road climbs to the
Marangu Gate of the Kilimanjaro
National Park (1,980 metres).
Guides and porters: the use of
authorized guides and porters is
obligatory. The hotels in Marangu
are the most expert trekking
organizers in the area. Alternatively
you can try at Moshi or Arusha.
Detours and peaks: the Umbwe
and Shira routes are easy but steeper
than those of Machame and
Marangu. The Uhuru Peak (5,895
metres), the highest in Africa,

is on all the trekking itineraries.
The ascent of Mawenzi (5,148
metres) is a mountaineering route
on ice and rock.
In case of trouble: on the Marangu
route guides and porters can
evacuate any injured persons
on wheeled stretchers quickly.
The isolation of the Machame route
makes it more difficult.
Maps: the best are the *Walkers'
Guide and Map of Kilimanjaro*
by M. Savage, or the *D.O.S. Map
of Kilimanjaro*. Both are on a scale
of 1:50,000.
Guidebooks: those happy with
brief details can choose the above
mentioned *Walkers' Guide and Map
of Kilimanjaro* or the small guide
book *Kilimanjaro National Park*
published by the National Park
Department of Tanzania.
Itineraries on Kilimanjaro are
described in numerous publications
including the *Guide to Mount Kenya
and Kilimanjaro* by Iain Allen
(Mountain Club of Kenya, 1982),
the *East Africa International
Mountain Guide* by Andrew
Wielochowski (West Col, 1986)
and *Backpacker's Africa - East and
Southern* by Hilary Bradt (Bradt-
Hunter, 1989).
For further reading: before leaving
you can read the hefty *Sui ghiacciai
dell'Africa* by Mario Fantin (Cappelli,
1968), *Snowcaps on the Equator*
by G. Boy, I. Allan and C. Ward
(The Bodley Head, 1988) or
Kilimanjaro by John Reader
(Elm Tree Books, 1989).
Naturalists are recommended
National Parks of East Africa by
J.G. Williams (Collins, 1981)
or *Kenya and Tanzania* by H.
and W. Hagen (Zanichelli, 1983).

THE MARANGU ROUTE

FIRST DAY
from the Marangu Gate
to the Mandara Hut
distance climbed: 870 metres
time: 4 hours

Undemanding, pleasant and tranquil, the first day of the trek is devoted to the splendid forest surrounding the base of the mountain. From the Park Gate you walk amid the mighty trunks of the podocarps and Macaranga kilimanjarica, interspersed with junipers and wild olive trees; here you will hear the shrill cries of the colobus and other species of monkeys.
It is, instead, quite unusual to spy the small forest antelopes such as the duiker. The path is all broad and easy. In the central section you can choose between two different routes, the final stretch is a little steeper.
The large (200 beds) and comfortable Mandara Hut (2,750 metres) stands on a splendid grassy clearing.

SECOND DAY
from the Mandara Hut
to the Horombo Hut
distance climbed: 1,020 metres
time: 4 hours

After leaving the rain forest, the path climbs gently through the magnificent, majestic tree-like heathers and you may come across the graceful flowers of the *Protea kilimanjarica*. After just over half an hour you will emerge onto open ground in sight of Kibo.
You continue at length on a fairly tiring and monotonous path that descends to cross many streams.
In the end you will reach the spacious and comfortable Horombo Hut (3,720 metres). About halfway along the central section, a marked path permits a detour to the interesting adventitious cone of the Maundi Crater (1 hour extra). At dawn and at sunset the view from the refuge hut towards Kibo is stunning. You should definitely stay two nights at the Horombo Hut to favour acclimatization. In this case you can go as far as the base of Mawenzi.

136 top Just below 3,000 metres, at the exit from the rain forest, the trekkers on the Marangu route find the Kibo glaciers (left) and the Mawenzi rocks before them.
Photograph by Marco Majrani

136 centre At the end of the first day trekkers spend the night in the comfortable Mandara Hut.
Photograph by Marco Majrani

136 bottom A pleasant half hour's walk from the village of Marangu is an attractive and spectacular water fall immersed in the forest.
Photograph by Stefano Ardito

136-137 Before reaching the Horombo Hut the large Marangu Path winds through magnificent groundsel.
Photograph by Marco Majrani

137 bottom left
The first leg of the
Marangu route will
amaze the trekker.
for a splendid
Macaranga and
podocarp forest.
Photograph by
Marco Majrani

137 bottom right
The Kibo crater and
its hanging glaciers
are a backdrop to
the Horombo Hut,
the largest on
Kilimanjaro that can
accommodate more
than 200 people.
Photograph by
Marco Majrani

138 top left
The path crossing the desolate Sella clearing leads trekkers to the Kibo Hut. In the background are the rocky peaks of Mawenzi.
Photograph by Marco Majrani

138 centre left
The trekkers that cross the Sella clearing have the unmistakable outline of Mount Kibo before them for the whole day.
Photograph by Stefano Amantini/ Atlantide

THIRD DAY
from the Horombo Hut to the Kibo Hut
distance climbed: 980 metres
time: 4 hours 30 minutes

After leaving the high trunk vegetation behind, you will enter the moonlike landscape of the Sella, the singular upland plain separating Kibo from Mawenzi. The path climbs with a limited gradient, passes the last spring (large notice board) and then looks (4,400 metres approximately) onto the Sella; you cross this for more than 4 kilometres towards Kibo, on the sides of which you will see the path climbing to the crater.
A last short climb leads to the Kibo Hut (4,703 metres) built in the traditional masonry of Alpine refuge huts.

138 botton left
The Kibo Hut is the last refuge hut before the climb to the summit along the Marangu route. The departure from the refuge starts at one a.m.
Photograph by Marco Majrani

138 right
From Horombo Hut those with an extra day can reach the base of the spectacular rocky Mawenzi pinnacles.
Photograph by Stefano Amantini/ Atlantide

139 top The steps of ice on the northern side of the crater can be seen from the path between Gillman's Point and Uhuru Peak.
Photograph by Marco Majrani

139 centre
From the 5,895 metres of Uhuru Peak, the light of dawn allows the eyes to sweep the lovely, large Mount Kibo crater, snowcapped for much of the year.
Photograph by Stefano Ardito

139 bottom
A Kilimanjaro guide stops at the foot of the charming, characteristic steps of ice between the Stella and Uhuru Peaks.
Photograph by Stefano Ardito

FOURTH DAY
from the Kibo Hut to the Uhuru Peak and descent to the Horombo Hut
distance climbed: 1,190 metres
distance descended: 2,170 metres
time: 10-14 hours

The crucial day, that leading to the peak, starts very early, usually between midnight and 1 a.m. A broad, clear path rises between enormous blocks of lava to reach the Hans Meyer Cave (5,150 metres) where the first

climbers camped in 1889. Past the cave comes the hardest part of the climb: a steep slope of fine volcanic gravel that the path climbs in wide bends. At the end of this, usually with the very first light of morning, you will arrive to the rocks of Gillman's Point (5,665 metres) on the edge of the crater. All that remains is to continue the far more gentle climb along the edge of the Kibo caldera. Skirt the Bismarck Towers, pass alongside the snowy Stella Point and, lastly, up a wide crest of snow or detritus that leads to the Uhuru Peak (5,895 metres). The descent returns the same way to the Kibo Hut and the Horombo Hut. The screes, interminable on the way up, will take just half an hour this time.

FIFTH DAY

from the Horombo Hut to Marangu
distance descended: 1,820 metres
time: 6 hours

After reaching the top you return to the starting point. On the descent, without the anxiety and fatigue of the ascent, you can admire the splendid forest between the Mandara Hut and the Marangu Gate.

THE MACHAME ROUTE

FIRST DAY
from the Machame Gate
to the Machame Hut
distance climbed: 1,350 metres
time: 4 hours

The loveliest and most complete route to the Kibo peak starts from the village of Machame, reached on the Moshi-Arusha road. The bureaucratic formalities must nonetheless be completed at the Marangu Gate and this inevitably means a start on foot in the afternoon, with the risk of being caught in a shower. You can even camp near the Machame Gate and leave on foot the following morning. From the Gate (1,950 metres) the path climbs with a gradual gradient and a never tiring route in a forest full of flowers (numerous *Impatiens pseudoviola* and *Impatiens kilimanjari*). A last ramp leads to the lovely rocky rise and the metal constructions of the Machame Hut (3,300 metres).

SECOND DAY
from the Machame Hut
to the Shira Hut
distance climbed: 500 metres
distance descended: 100 metres
time: 3 hours

A rather short day although the altitude begins to make itself felt. The path rises with a charming route along a lava ridge that offers splendid views of the Kibo and Meru peaks before crossing a number of clearings surrounded by very high, tree-like heathers. A stony stretch with the odd zigzag leads to the edge of the remarkable lava plateau of Shira. Cross this to the refuge hut of the same name (3,700 metres) near which there is a large cave.

140 top left On the less busy Machame route the first leg is again devoted to the passage through the beautiful dense forest at between 2,000 and 3,300 metres.
Photograph by Marco Majrani

140 centre left Before the Shira Hut the path on the Machame route includes some steep but easy rocks.
Photograph by Stefano Ardito

140 left bottom At 3,950 metres the Barranco Hut is a splendid viewpoint over the wildest side of Mount Kibo. Water falls and streams of ice streak the dark Breach Wall; to its right is the Heim Glacier.
Photograph by Stefano Ardito

140 right Just above the Machame Hut the path climbs through heather and lobelia and offers a good view of the distant pyramid of Mount Meru (4,566 metres).
Photograph by Stefano Ardito

THIRD DAY

from the Shira Hut
to the Barranco Hut
distance climbed: 700 metres
distance descended: 450 metres
time: 4 hours 30 minutes

This stage, quite tiring at first, explains why hikers starting from Machame suffer the altitude less on the final stage to the Kibo summit. Zigzagging up and down is, on any mountain, the best way to get acclimatized.
You start by reaching an enormous solitary rock and then proceed on wide, desolate, stony slopes towards the Lava Tower and the Arrow Glacier Hut. High up, in the distance are the walls of the Western Breach. Once at the ridge at the base of the Lava Tower (4,400 metres approximately) a steep descent leads to the Barranco Hut (3,950 metres), a splendid viewpoint of the Breach Wall and the Heim and Decken glaciers. All around are magnificent specimens of giant groundsels.

FOURTH DAY

from the Barranco Hut
to the Barafu Hut
distance climbed: 750 metres
distance descended: 200 metres
time: 5 hours

A long and spectacular day preceding the ascent to the summit. You start by crossing the Barranco Valley and climbing beyond it via a number of easy rock passages. Once at the broad, rocky ridge that affords a wonderful view of the Heim glacier, you descend rapidly into the Karanga Valley, stopping beside a huge cave to stock up on firewood and water. The last stretch of the climb follows a rocky wind-beaten ridge and leads to the two constructions of the Barafu Hut (4,500 metres).

141 top The light of dawn sees a party crossing the flat snowfields of the Kibo crater towards the Uhuru Peak.
Photograph by Stefano Ardito

141 centre Smaller and far less comfortable than the large refuge huts on the Marangu route, the Barafu Hut (4,600 metres) accommodates the trekker for the night preceding the climb to the Kibo summit via the Machame route. Once again the departure is in the middle of the night.
Photograph by Stefano Ardito

141 bottom A few minutes' hike from the Uhuru Peak, Kilmanjaro's white steps of ice contrast with the black scree of volcanic origin.
Photograph by Marco Majrani

FIFTH DAY

from the Barafu Hut to the Uhuru Peak and the Horombo Hut
distance climbed: 1,490 metres
distance descended: 2,170 metres
time: 10-14 hours

Again, the day devoted to the peak starts just after midnight. Leaving the refuge hut, a good path marked by stones climbs the rocky slopes and into the wide gorge to the right (east) of the Rebmann glacier. A section on more friable ground - nothing like the screes of Gillman's Point! - precedes the last slopes, generally covered with snow. Despite the modest gradient, these are often iced over before dawn: an ice axe and crampons can make progress safer. Once out on the crater at Stella Point (5,750 metres) you go left to the Uhuru Peak (5,895 metres). To descend, follow the crater to Gillman's Point then continue along the normal route to the Kibo Hut and the Horombo Hut. Here you will find your porters who come from the Barafu Hut via a path across the mountainside.

SIXTH DAY

from the Horombo Hut
to the Marangu gate
distance descended: 1,820 metres
time: 6 hours

The descent is along the crowded Marangu route. For those who took a different route on the way up, this stretch of forest will be of particular interest. Once at the Mandara Hut you proceed without difficulty to the Marangu Gate.

FISH RIVER CANYON

In the untamed heart of Namibia

142-143 This splendid photograph shows the great, multicoloured setting that Fish River created by erosion over thousands of years. Photograph by Marc van Aarst

Situated in the southernmost corner of Namibia, Fish River Canyon is one of the greatest - and least known to visitors from America or Europe - of the natural wonders of Africa. 160 kilometres long, up to 25 wide and on average 500 metres deep, this remarkable gorge dug by a tributary of the Orange River is the second largest on earth after the Grand Canyon in Colorado. Just like its big brother in America, Fish River Canyon is both an open-air geological museum and an extraordinary adventure terrain. Often admired from above by tourists in cars stopping to admire the breathtaking panorama of the canyon from the viewpoints built on the eastern bank, Fish River (Vis River in Afrikaans) offers the hiker one of the most fascinating treks of the whole African continent; this trek through a wild, spectacular environment rich in surprises will take approx. four days.

Roughly 80 kilometres long, because of the climate this trek can only be made in the heart of the austral winter (i.e. from early May to the end of August) and by those presenting the rangers with a certificate of physical fitness at the entrance. For safety reasons access to the path is allowed only to groups of at least three hikers. To reduce the environmental impact, not more than 40 people can use the path per day.

It is therefore best to book although small groups can reasonably hope that some trekkers with bookings will not show up.

The first and main reason for the interest of this path are the bizarre rock formations and the singular grandeur of the walls that close the sides of the canyon. These have interspersed layers of sandstone, calcareous rock, schist and granite. Characteristic and highly attractive are also the intrusions of dolerite, a basaltic rock. The close presence of the river

is unusual and exciting; flowing for 760 kilometres it is the longest in Namibia and one of the few to contain fish.

Considering the harsh desert climate, there is an abundance of land fauna in the area. In the Fish River Conservation Area it is not unusual to encounter springboks, klipspringers, Hartman mountain zebras and hyrax. Baboons are rather numerous but the leopard, the lord of the savannah, wil only allow himself to be sighted in exceptional circumstances. More than 60 species of birds have been catalogued around Ai-Ais. Easily seen from the bottom of the canyon are vultures and eagles gliding on the hot air that rises from the depths of the valley bottom. Among the species of special interest to the birdwatcher-hiker are the African black duck *(Anas sparsa)*, the Cape robin *(Cossypha caffra)*, the grey heron and the hamerkop *(Scopus umbretta)*, a characteristic brown-coloured wading bird common all over southern Africa. Beside pools of stagnant water on the banks of the Fish River you will often spot the Monitor of the Nile, a large but peaceloving lizard known in Namibia with the native name of *leguaan*.

Flora is rather scarce, limited by the torrid desert climate to a few species of succulents. On the bottom of the canyon cyclical floods prevent the growth of high trunk plants; these manage to grow in the deep secondary valleys descending towards Fish River and here you may come across ebony and acacia trees.

The same species find some living space in the main valley where it broadens - south of Sulphur Springs. Everywhere the most common plant is the *Euphorbia gregoria*, flanked by various other prickly species common to desert climes.

Although isolated and wild, the canyon Fish River runs through has been known to man since very distant times. According to the San, one of the primitive desert peoples, the canyon was created by the snake Koutelga Kooru when it withdrew here into a deep den to escape the hunters chasing it. The Ai-Ais thermal springs owe their name to the Khoikhoi. In their language this word means "boiling". The southernmost tribes of the Nama people travelled these barren valleys in search of wildlife and here they had a bitter skirmish with the German colonial army. On the path following the valley bottom those difficult days are commemorated with the tomb of Lieutenant Thilo von Trotha, killed during a clash at the point where the Goschadrift flows into Fish River.

The need to conserve this magnificent area was acknowledged in 1962 when the canyon came under protection as a national monument. In 1965 a wildlife reserve was created around Ai-Ais and in 1969 the whole area became a splendid national park covering slightly more than 49,000 hectares. This dimension was greatly multiplied twenty years later with the institution of the Ai-Ais Conservation Area, an outstanding protected area of more than 346,000 hectares that includes the solitary and almost unknown Huns Mountains that rise to the west of Fish River and offer a landscape that has by many travellers been compared to that of the Moon.

USEFUL INFORMATION

Duration: 5 days, although trained groups can take 5-6 days.
Elevation: from 250 to 950 metres
Period: the trek is open and accessible from 1 May to 31 August every year.
Red tape: No visa is required for Namibia. The Fish River Canyon Trek must however be booked some time in advance with the Reservations Office, Nature Conservation and Recreation Resorts, Private Bag 13267 Windhoek 9000 or by telephoning (00264)(61)236975. Sometimes a permit can be obtained at the last minute by joining another group or taking advantage of a cancellation. A certificate of good physical fitness issued 40 days before the start of the trek is also required.
Degree of difficulty: no technical problems but beware of the climate as temperatures may exceed 40°C even in winter months. The ground alternates rock and sand and can be awkward especially in the first section of the trek and causes numerous hikers to give up and climb up the path that starts just before Sulphur Springs. When the river level is high the numerous (twenty or so in all) crossings from one bank to the other become proper fords.
Physical challenge: average-high because of the torrid climate, difficult terrain and the bulk of the rucksack.
Equipment: normal trekking gear. A tent and adequate food supplies are required. A hook and line for fishing in Fish River are useful (and permitted). The river water is drinkable and anyway it is the only water available.
Access routes: the Fish River Conservation Area is just over 120 kilometres from Grünau, 165 kilometres from Keetmanshoop and 259 from Springbok on the road between Windhoek, the South African border and Cape Town. It is hard to reach by public transport: buses run only on the road between Windhoek, Springbok and Cape Town. Hitchhiking from here to the canyon is difficult because of the scarce traffic. Groups of trekkers must register at Ai-Ais before

144 top Fish River Canyon offers an extraordinary spectacle to the traveller in southern Namibia. Photograph by Mauro Burzio

144 bottom At the end of the austral summer the bed of Fish River is completely dry and the trek loses some of its fascination. Photograph by KBA

travelling the 65 kilometres to the northernmost viewpoint where the path commences.

Guides and porters: some agencies in Windhoek or Cape Town offer organized guided treks along the canyon. There are no porters.

Detours and peaks: the route is obligatory and is indicated by the river. The only possible variation is the path climbing towards the bank from Sulphur Springs which can be used as an escape route.

In case of trouble: a path leads up towards the eastern bank of the canyon about an hour north of Sulphur Springs. In case of accident evacuation by helicopter can be requested although it is anything but economical.

Maps: there are no good maps available.

Guidebooks: the *Visitor's Guide to Namibia* by Willie and Sandra Olivier (Southern Books, 1989) is useful.

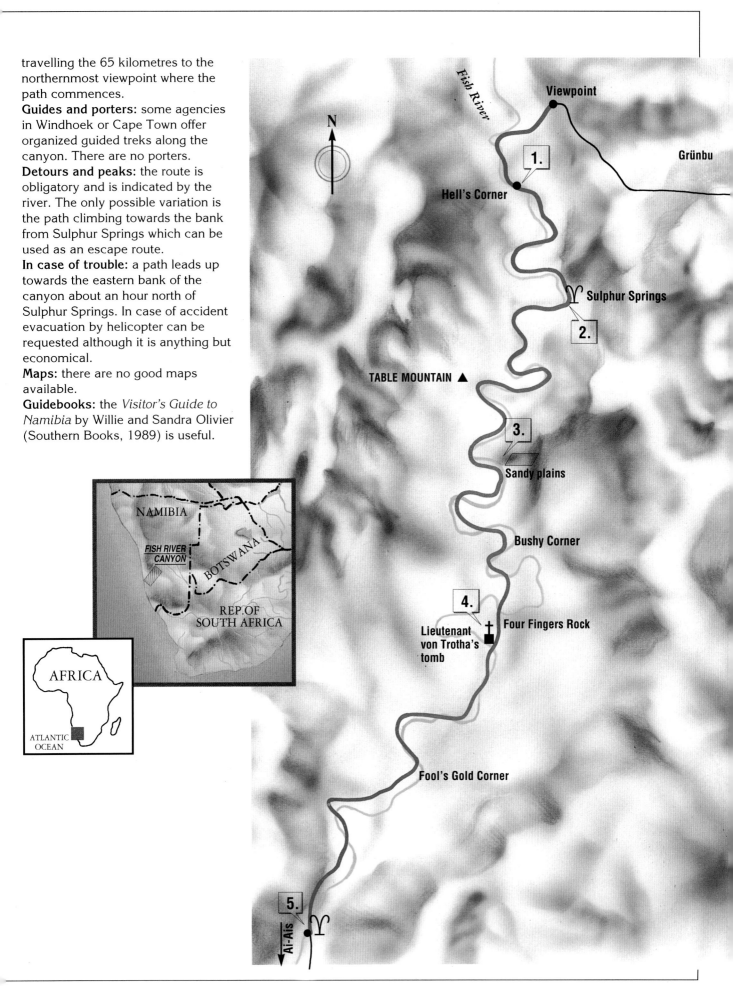

FIRST DAY
*from the northernmost viewpoint
to Hell's Corner
distance climbed: 50 metres
distance descended: 600 metres
time: 5 hours*

A fairly short day on which even those arriving quite late in the canyon can acclimatize without too much difficulty. Those leaving very early can try to cover a greater distance and reach Sulphur Springs on the first stage. The hike starts from the northernmost viewpoint on Fish River from where a steep and exposed path, in some parts equipped with metal chains, will enable you to make 600 metres of distance descended in approximately 1 hour and come to the bottom of the valley.
From here on the route is clear and follows the many bends of the valley plunging into its narrowest and wildest parts (Hell's Corner). After a characteristic outcrop of dolerite you can choose among the numerous places to camp.

SECOND DAY
*from Hell's Corner
to Sulphur Springs
distance climbed: 50 metres
distance descended: 100 metres
time: 5 hours*

Another not particularly long day on which you have to come to terms with the still awkward and tiring terrain. Continue without ever leaving the river and passing another two outcrops of dolerite. Slightly past the last of these, on the left, is a path that can be used as an escape route. Follow the valley southwards to Sulphur Springs and an inviting group of palm trees.

THIRD DAY
*from Sulphur Springs
to the sandy plain
distance climbed: 50 metres
distance descended: 100 metres
time: 6 hours*

Once past Sulphur Springs, the canyon starts to broaden and the

rocks and fine sand of the first stage give way to a stony, easier terrain. The path continues along the banks of the river, following a less winding stretch of the valley and then comes to another series of impressive meanders dominated on the eastern side (right for the hiker) by the steep rocky spurs of the Table Mountain; the shape of this will remind hikers from Cape Town of the mountain at home. Camp farther on in a magnificent and characteristic sandy plain right at the foot of the canyon's rocky walls.

FOURTH DAY
from the sandy plain
to von Trotha's tomb
distance climbed: 150 metres
distance descended: 200 metres
time: 6 hours

Leaving the sandy plain behind you proceed along another interminable meander to an area richer in vegetation (Bushy Corner); follow another meander and leave the river bed for the path that takes a shortcut across a promontory on the western side. Cross Fish River within sight of a characteristic group of towers (Four Fingers Rock) and then take another longer shortcut returning to Fish River a short distance from the tomb of the German Lieutenant Thilo von Trotha.

FIFTH DAY
from von Trotha's tomb to Ai-Ais
distance climbed: 100 metres
distance descended: 150 metres
time: 7 hours

Quite long but on fairly trouble-free terrain, this fifth and last stage of the trek will lead you directly to a relaxing and enjoyable bathe in the thermal springs of Ai-Ais. An almost straight section of the valley leads to a lovely slab of basaltic rock and farther on Fool's Gold Corner and a settlement in ruin. At the end, where the walls of the canyon lower and lose their majesty, comes Ai-Ais.

146 top
The northern viewpoint, one of the most spectacular in the Fish River Conservation Area, offers a splendid view of the river and lovely valley. Photograph by Hein von Horsten/A.B.P.L.

146 centre Before commencing the steep descent to the banks of the river, a trekker stops to look down on the deep furrow of Fish River Canyon. Photograph by Hein von Horsten/A.B.P.L.

146 bottom Two antelope seem to pose for the photographer on the edge of the canyon. Photograph by Camerapix

147 top A trekker follows the left bank of Fish River beside the thick vegetation present in spite of the canyon's torrid desert climate. Photograph by KBA

147 centre top A trekker stops before one of the many (twenty or so in all) passages from one side of Fish River to the other; these sometimes become fords proper when the river level is high. Photograph by Hein von Horsten/A.B.P.L.

147 centre bottom The temperatures are extremely high in the middle of the day and trekkers should exploit the cool hours of dawn. Photograph by Hein von Horsten/A.B.P.L.

147 bottom The comfortable and convenient Ai-Ais thermal springs offer a well deserved rest after the exhausting crossing of the canyon. Photograph by Roger de La Harpe/A.B.P.L.

THROUGH THE CEDARBERGS

Wilderness and leopard trails in the
mountains of Cape Province

The noisy colonies of marine birds at Lambert's Bay and Langebaan, the Namaqualand flowers that seem suddenly to colour the desert. Plantations of citrus fruit and roads deviating towards the coast, bizarre-shaped rocks and unlimited expanses of the plateau. Among the many magnificent roads in South Africa that running six hundred and more kilometres from Cape Town to the banks of the Orange River and the border with Namibia is, for the nature enthusiast, an uninterrupted succession of emotions, landscapes and places to see.

For the first hour of the journey the mountains of "Hottentot Holland" close the horizon to the east. For the second the groves of oranges, lemons and grapefruit lend a green hue to a landscape that gradually becomes more barren. Then, the course of the Olifants River widens into the great artificial lake of Clanwilliam and more rocks rise to dominate the road. To the right, for those arriving from the Cape, the horizon is filled by a chain of mountains of a harsh stony Mediterranean appearance. Before reaching this, however, there is another half hour's journey along the dusty dirt track that connects the splendid Cape Dutch architecture of Clanwilliam to the forest station of Algeria and the entrance to the protected area (a Wilderness Area, not a Park) of the mountains.

Well loved by hikers from all over Cape Province, the Cedarberg chain culminates in the 2,028 metres of Sneeuberg, an elongated rocky ridge that may even be snowclad in the coldest days of the austral winter. Better known among hikers and travellers are the unusual rock formations - including the Maltese Cross and Wolfsberg Arch - that rise suddenly from the plateau. Unexpectedly, among the rocks appear small, retiring populations of baboons and antelopes such as the klipspringer and the rhebok although

reptiles and the birds of prey that cross the sky incessantly are seen more frequently. Only the prints, trails in exceptional cases, reveal the presence of the caracal, the Cape fox, and the dozen or so leopards still living in the heart of these isolated mountains.

However harsh and primeval they may appear to the traveller of today, the Cedarberg landscape has been profoundly changed by man. When, in 1661, Jan Dunckert was the first white man to cross this part of the Cape Province he told of the extensive and fragrant cedar forests *(Widdringtonia cedarbergensis)* and so named the mountains.

A hundred years later the wood-cutters were already at work in many parts of the Cedarbergs, as is obvious from the network of paved paths and muletracks that today make life easier for those walking for fun. Not until 1876 were the rangers ordered to control felling.

Today the woods that gave their name to the Cedarbergs have completely disappeared in many parts of the range. A visit to these mountains and the Cedarberg Wilderness Area protecting them should not be only a trek based on regret and silent condemnation of the umpteenth environmental catastrophe caused by the white man in Africa. The singular outlines of the rocks, the caves with their ancient drawings, the isolated farms in the heart of a solitary and eerie landscape move even those visiting the area for just a few hours.

Hikes of a few hours, accessible without any special formalities, will take you to the bizarre and spectacular silhouettes of the Maltese Cross, Wolfberg's Arch and the other best known rocky formations. Those intent on longer hikes must, however, keep to the rules - severe as all over South Africa - of the Cedarberg Wilderness Area. Unlike the national parks, there are no obligatory routes.

Only 50 people per day are allowed onto the paths of each of the three sections into which the 71,000 hectares of the protected area have been divided. It is best to book for weekends in spring and autumn, when the flow to the area is at a maximum, to avoid unpleasant surprises and biting disappointments.

150 Magnificent, colourful blossoms enliven the Namaqualand steppes at the beginning of the austral spring, between the end of August and the end of September. This is the best season for a visit to the Cedarbergs. Photograph by Colla Swart/ A.B.P.L.

A little care is needed when choosing the best moment to hike in the area. The scorching sun of the austral summer, from December to March, turns the plateau and Cedarberg peaks into a red-hot and inhospitable expanse, suited only to those with much experience in hiking in the harshest climates of Africa.
For most trekkers the middle seasons are certainly the most convenient time to tackle the chain. The winter, often very cold on the Cedarbergs, offers crystal-clear air and an encounter with the snow protea (Protea cryophila) one of the rarest and most touching plants on the continent.
The trek described here is rather long but not over-tiring and will bring you in contact with some of the most characteristic landscapes of the range; it includes an ascent of Sneeuberg (2,028 metres) and Tafelberg (1,968 metres), the two highest peaks in the Cedarberg chain and in the whole Cape Province. Even in the mild South African winters it is not unusual to find traces of snow here.
The first ascent is very easy, the second includes a rock climb on the limit between second and third degree and non-mountaineers will certainly prefer to be secured with a piece of rope. The Tafelberg ascent is of considerable interest even if you stop at the base of the chimney that leads to the top. Sneeukop (1,930 metres) can be added to the first two peaks; this is the third highest peak in the chain. It goes without saying that the physical demands of the trek are more than slightly reduced if the climb to the summits is eliminated. The most graceful peak in the Cedarbergs is, however, another. On the very first day of the trek, at the end of the not tiring climb from the ford on the Dwarsrivier, the trekker will find himself before the Maltese Cross, a charming pinnacle about forty metres high and in the characteristic form of a cross. Popular among the Cape climbers despite its modest dimensions and the length of the approach, this rock offers a remarkable spectacle, especially at sunset.
Those forgoing the ascent of the Sneeuberg will be able to admire it almost until the sun goes down, before starting out on the plateau for the not distant Sneeuberg Hut.

USEFUL INFORMATION

Duration: 5 days, easily reduced to four.
Elevation: from the 580 metres of Algeria to the 2,028 of Sneeuberg.
Period: all year round but the best and recommended periods are without doubt autumn and spring. Hikers accustomed to the European climates will have no trouble in tackling the Cedarbergs in winter (from June to August). The austral summer is truly scorching.
Red tape: for treks of more than one day a hiking permit must be booked with the Chief Nature Conservator, Private Bag XI, Citrusdal 7340, or telephone Flemlian (0027)(27) 4822812. Permits can be collected at the forest station of Algeria.
Degree of difficulty: the only technical problems of the trek (a chimney between second and third degree) are on the climb to Tafelberg and can easily be avoided. Care should be taken with the sun, unrelenting in the central hours of the day, and with paths that are not always clearly marked.

Physical challenge: average
Equipment: normal trekking gear. Sleeping bag, mattress and stove are required for any nights in the refuge huts and caves found along the way. A tent is necessary only if the huts are occupied by rangers or researchers. The best solution is to take it with you to Algeria, then decide whether or not to put it in your rucksack. No fires may be lit in the open air inside the protected area.
Access routes: Clanwilliam is approximately 200 kilometres from Cape Town on the road to Springbok and Namibia. From here a wide clear dirt track leads in 15 kilometres to the forest station of Algeria (580 metres) and proceeds inside the Cedarberg Wilderness Area to reach, after 13 kilometres, the Cedarberg farm (870 metres). There are bus services as far as Clanwilliam but after the town you must continue on foot or hitchhike.
Guides and porters: there are none.
Detours and peaks: the two principal peaks of the Cedarbergs are on the main route, from which Sneeukop (1,930 metres), the third highest summit on the range, can also be reached. An interesting variation goes from Sanddrif to the Welbedacht Cave, passing Wolfberg's Arch, another well known rock formation of considerable attraction.
In case of trouble: along the route it is possible to ask for help at the Cedarberg farm and the forest stations of Welbedacht and Algeria. All three are on the road crossing the chain from north to south.
Maps: the best is the Cedarbergs in scale 1:50,000 published by the Forestry Department.
Guidebooks: an itinerary in the Cedarbergs is described in Best Hikes in South Africa by David Bristow (Struik Publications, 1992). Also useful is The Guide to Backpacking and Wilderness Areas by Sandra and Willie Olivier (Southern Book Publishers, 1989).
For further reading: among the most interesting works is Mountains of Southern Africa by D. Bristow and C. Ward (Struik, 1985).

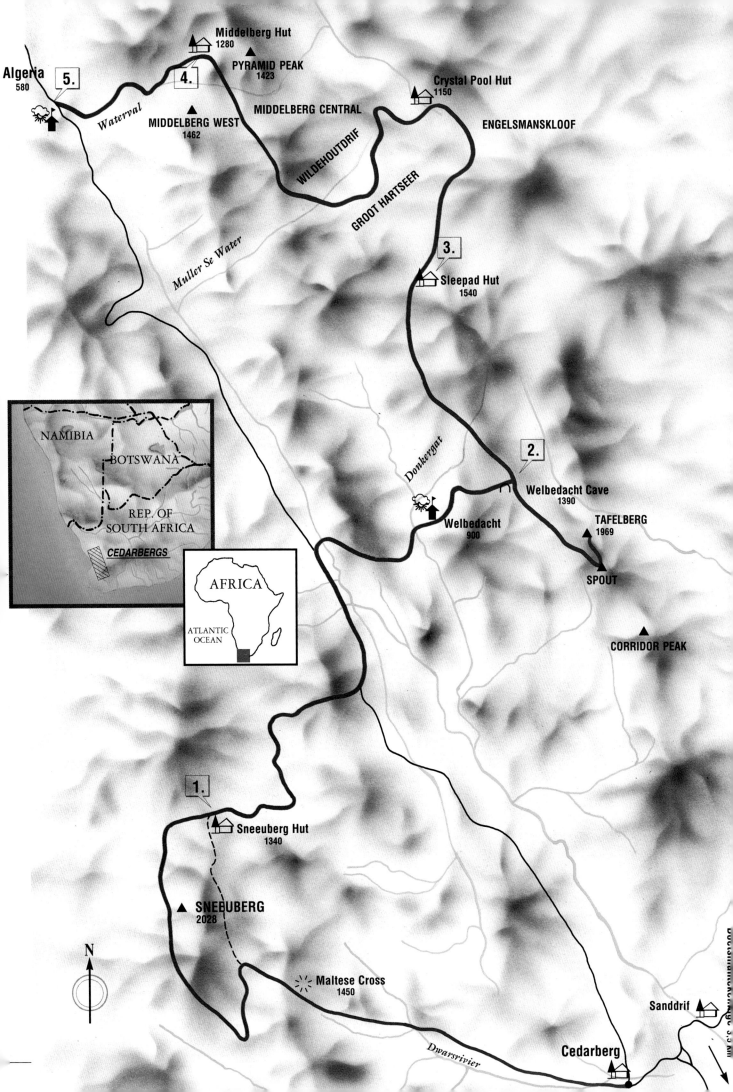

Middelberg Hut
1280

PYRAMID PEAK
1423

Algeria
580

5.

4.

Waterval

MIDDELBERG WEST
1462

MIDDELBERG CENTRAL

WILDEHOUTDRIF

Crystal Pool Hut
1150

ENGELSMANSKLOOF

GROOT HARTSEER

Muller Se Water

3.

Sleepad Hut
1540

NAMIBIA

BOTSWANA

REP. OF
SOUTH AFRICA

CEDARBERGS

Donkergat

2.

Welbedacht Cave
1390

TAFELBERG
1969

Welbedacht
900

SPOUT

AFRICA

ATLANTIC
OCEAN

CORRIDOR PEAK

1.

Sneeuberg Hut
1340

Sanddrif

▲ SNEEUBERG
2028

N

Maltese Cross
1450

Dwarsrivier

Cedarberg

FIRST DAY
*from Cedarberg Farm to Sneeuberg
and the Sneeuberg Hut
distance climbed: 1,100 metres
distance descended: 720 metres
time: 6 hours*

At the south-western corner of the Cedarbergs, the farm of the same name (850 metres) is the starting point for the trek and for many shorter excursions. Those who reach this area the day before should pay a visit to the rock drawings at Boetsmantekeninge, 3.5 kilometres south of the farm along the track leading to the Matjesrivier farm. From the same track, after approximately one kilometre, a detour leads to the Sanddrif farm where you can camp or rent a bungalow. Back at the Cedarberg farm follow the track winding for little more than 3 kilometres to the base of the Sneeuberg massif. After fording the Dwarsrivier, a good path indicated by little mounds enters a rocky ravine climbing it to the plain and the splendid Maltese Cross (1,450 metres), one of the best known rock formations in South Africa. Proceed on the plateau and then fork left climbing to the large top ridge that leads to the right to the Sneeuberg peak (2,028 metres). Descend along the northern ridge to a plateau from where, to the left, you will reach the Sneeuberg Hut (1,340 metres). A straight path will bring you here from the Maltese Cross in just over an hour.

SECOND DAY
*from the Sneeuberg Hut to the
Welbedacht Cave
distance climbed: 550 metres
distance descended: 480 metres
time: 3 hours 30 minutes*

Not a long but an interesting stage on which you will move from the western to the eastern sector of the Cedarbergs, crossing the road leading to the starting point of the trek. From the refuge hut follow the cart-track crossing westwards and descending to the bottom of a valley, leaving it to cross northwards again and then descending to the road (910 metres) that crosses the Cedarbergs. Follow this to the left for 2 kilometres and then turn right; after another 2 kilometres you will reach the forest station of Welbedacht (900 metres) which occupies an abandoned farm. After leaving the Driehoek River Valley, a path climbs through the characteristic rock formations. Just before you emerge onto a plateau crossed by a dirt track you will come to Welbedacht Cave (1,390 metres), a large cave overlooking the river that runs through the valley. Those reaching this point around lunch-time will manage to climb Tafelberg in the afternoon and continue the next day to the Crystal Pool Hut: this shortens the trek by 1 day.

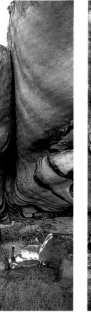

*152 top left
The brightly
coloured rocks
in the Cedarberg
region suggest
a fanciful artist
who has gone mad
with his brush.
Photograph by
Mauro Burzio*

*152 top right
A trekker observes
some rock drawings
near the
Boetsmantekeninge
rocks.
Photograph by
Stefano Ardito*

*152 centre As well
as the best known
rock formations,
dozens of other
spectacular rock
towers overlook the
steppe and high
Cedarberg valleys.
Photograph by Hein
Von Horsten/A.B.P.L.*

THIRD DAY

from the Welbedacht Cave
to Tafelberg and the Sleepad Hut
distance climbed: 820 metres
distance descended: 670 metres
time: 6 hours

From the cave, where it is wise to leave most of your belongings, a short hike will take you to the dirt track (1,430 metres) that crosses Die Trap, the flat belt breaking up the Cedarberg slopes. Follow this briefly to the right and then leave it to climb crossways towards the clearly visible Tafelberg rocks, flanked on the right by the characteristic Spout, a name justified by the fact that the whole mountain looks like a teapot. After reaching the little saddle between the Spout and Tafelberg take a steep rocky ravine that terminates with a vertical chimney about ten metres high; this requires knowledge of climbing techniques. Beyond this passage (2nd-3rd degree) comes the top plateau (1,969 metres). Back at the cave follow the dirt track on the plain northwards again. After crossing the deep Donkergat river valley you will come to the Sleepad Hut (1,540 metres).

FOURTH DAY

from the Sleepad Hut
to the Middelberg Hut
distance climbed: 130 metres
distance descended: 390 metres
time: 5 hours

Pleasant and all zigzags, this day offers the trekker a considerable variety of environments and views as well as the opportunity to see protea, bamboo and the other rare botanic species that flourish beside the Muller se Water stream. From the Middelberg Hut you can descend in one day to the forest station of Algeria. Start out following Die Trap for about an hour; leave it to descend to the left (north) into the lovely, narrow rocky Engelsmanskloof valley. At the end of this veer right around the rocks and climb quickly to the Crystal Pool Hut (1,150 metres) which owes it name to the crystal clear spring encountered at the end of the subsequent descent. Start out again westwards with a long stretch on the flat and descend steeply along the Groot Hartseer ridge to the Wildehoutdrif and then the Muller se Water valleys, the latter definitely deserving a stop. A last climb leads to the Middelberg Hut (1,280 metres).

FIFTH DAY

from the Middelberg Hut to Algeria
distance descended: 650 metres
time: 1 hours 45 minutes

The last stage of the trek, very short, can be preceded by a brief climb (1 hour 30 minutes return) to the nearby peaks of Middelberg West (1,462 metres) and Pyramid Peak (1,423 metres) for a last glance towards the broad ridges of the Cedarbergs. After leaving the refuge hut you enter one of the last remaining cedar woods on the massif. A lovely stretch in the dense vegetation beside the waters of the Waterval precedes the last steep decent towards the bridge over the Rondegat river and the forest station of Algeria (580 metres), a clear pool nearby permitting a refreshing bathe after your toil.

152 bottom Easily reached also by tourists in cars, the Maltese Cross is one of the most striking and frequently photographed monoliths in South Africa.
Photograph by Hein Von Horsten/A.B.P.L.

153 top left Unusual rock formations rise near the Maltese Cross.
Photograph by Mauro Burzio

153 bottom left The trail coming from Clanwilliam and the forest station of Algeria crosses the desolate Driehoek River Valley, in the heart of the Cedarbergs.
Photograph by Mauro Burzio

153 top right A deep rocky valley opens suddenly between the Cedarberg rocks and plateaux.
Photograph by Mauro Burzio

153 bottom right Water is a precious and rare asset in the arid Cedarberg rocks.
Photograph by Mauro Burzio

THE OTTER TRAIL

On the wild Tsitsikamma coast

154-155 After leaving the Visitor Centre and the chalets of the Tsitsikamma National Park behind, *the first leg of the Otter Trail crosses a short flat strip not far from the cliffs.* **Photograph by Stefano Ardito**

The Tsitsikamma Park deserves a special mention amongst the thousand spectacles of nature and the great contrasts of the "South African planet".

On the southernmost coast of the continent, overlooking the stormy waters of the Indian Ocean, the coast included in the protected area is an incredible and fascinating succession of forests and cliffs, hidden beaches, river estuaries and natural scenic spots from where the gaze sweeps over the vast ocean and various species of whales often appear.

This is a two-three hours journey from Port Elizabeth and six-seven from Cape Town, at the foot of the Outeniqua mountains separating the humid and rainy coastal plain from the semi-desertic Great Karroo steppe. Colonized long ago, the plain is a tidy succession of crops and timber woods. Slightly west are the Knysna, Mossel Bay and Plettenberg Bay beaches, linked by the famous Garden Route and popular with bathers in the austral summer and all year round with sailing and windsurf enthusiasts. In our summer, the most exciting activity is whale watching as these mammals come to within a few dozen metres of the shore. Tsitsikamma is, however, the biggest surprise. After leaving the main road, a short detour amidst fields leads to the Park entrance and an incredible change in the landscape. On the side sloping down to the Ocean the rain forest is still beautifully intact and descends steep and compact towards the high cliffs and the crashing waves of the coast. Here between the rocky coast and the forest winds the exceptional South African Hiking Way System. In five days the Otter Trail provides a series of emotions and truly extraordinary views; depending on the period and presence or absence of sun, rain and wind, it is reminiscent of both the Mediterranean and Scotland. The fauna and flora are, however, typically South African. Crossed by streams and enriched by splendid undergrowth, the forest offers the nature lover beautiful species of trees, shrubs and ferns.

In the more open parts, there are numerous different species of protea, the magnificent plant symbol of the country.

The most interesting of the animal species - rarely seen because of its

155 Overlooking the stormy waters of the Indian Ocean, visitors marvel at the streams, ferns and moss in the splendid Tsitsikamma National Park forest. Photograph by Lanz Von Horsten/A.B.P.L.

Lottering Forest

BAKENKOP ▲

Bloukrans River

Bloukrans Forest

156 A truly spectacular waterfall just a few metres from the sea marks the boundary of the section of Otter Trail, accessible without any special formalities. A permit must be requested much in advance to continue from here to the Ngubu Hut. Photograph by Stefano Ardito

Klip River

André Hut   TSITSIKAMMA. NAT. PARK

MARTIENSE BANK

4.

NATURE'S VALLEY

5.

N

INDIAN

predominantly nocturnal habits - is the Cape otter *(Aonyx capensis)* to which this trek is devoted. A splendid creature, it can grow to one and a half metres in length and exceed 15 kilograms in weight; it feeds mainly on frogs, crabs and fish. Seventy kilometres long (but only 5 wide at the most) the Tsitsikamma National Park also protects a wide stretch of sea where fishing of any kind is prohibited. Officially established and organized in 1968, in the Seventies the Otter Trail soon became the most popular trek in South Africa. As the number of trekkers is limited to 12 per day, it must be booked at least a year in advance. This is certainly based on sound environmental grounds but makes the Otter Trail almost inaccessible to foreigners. Even without a booking, lovers of nature and hiking should not forget a visit to Tsitsikamma. Lapped by the waves and dominated by the dark rain forest, the most spectacular

coast in South Africa provides a series of lovely and interesting hikes on the nature paths around the deep Storms River estuary. Moreover, there are no particular formalities for the first stretch of the Otter Trail. This takes three-four hours return and makes it possible to become familiar with the dense coastal forest, the majestic rocky coast around Guano Cave and the lovely waterfalls two thirds of the way along the first stage. Far off, in the ocean, you can often sight whales. In the woods, with a little luck, you will spot some "duiker", the small, shy forest antelopes. On the rocky coast - and especially around the camp site and the Storms River Visitor Centre - you can see "hyrax", small quadrupeds resembling badgers but related to the elephant. For those familiar with the paths of Kilimanjaro and Mount Kenya, this encounter transports you abruptly from sea level to an altitude of four thousand metres.

USEFUL INFORMATION

Duration: 5 days.
Elevation: from 0 to 150 metres.
Period: all year round but the best months are between October and April.
Red tape: access to the Otter Trail is limited and it is the most coveted trek in the whole of South Africa. The trek must be booked at least a year in advance with the National Parks Board of Pretoria or Cape Town (P.O. Box 787 Pretoria 0001, tel. (0027) (12) 3431991, P.O. Box 7400 Roggebaai 8012, tel. (0027)(21) 2222810. A maximum of twelve persons are admitted per day.
Degree of difficulty: no technical problems. Great attention must be paid to river levels in case of heavy rain.
Physical challenge: average. The ascents and descents are

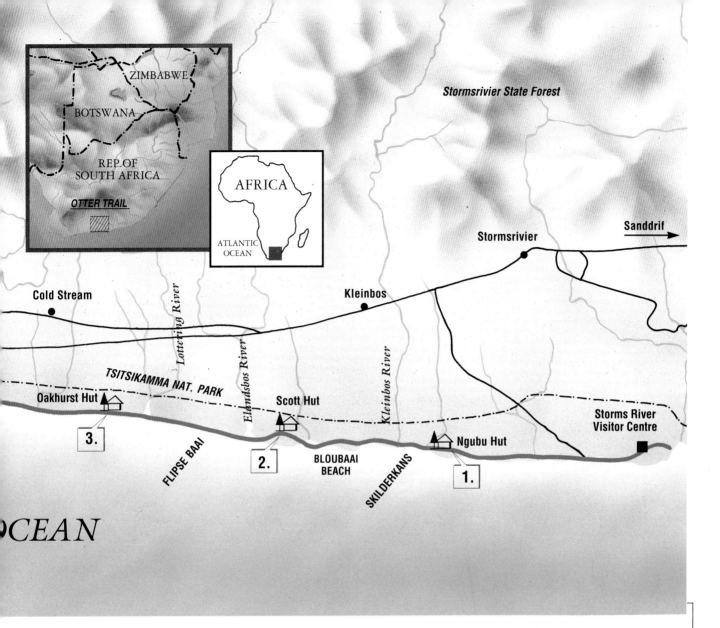

Stormsrivier State Forest

ZIMBABWE

BOTSWANA

REP. OF
SOUTH AFRICA

OTTER TRAIL

AFRICA

ATLANTIC
OCEAN

Sanddrif →

Cold Stream

Kleinbos

Stormsrivier

Lottering River

Elandsbos River

Kleinbos River

TSITSIKAMMA NAT. PARK

Oakhurst Hut

Scott Hut

3.

2.

FLIPSE BAAI

BLOUBAAI
BEACH

SKILDERKANS

Ngubu Hut

**Storms River
Visitor Centre**

1.

OCEAN

continuous although limited in range.
Equipment: normal trekking gear
with a good anorak, sleeping bag
and food for the duration of the trek.
The refuge huts have beds with
mattresses and stoves with a supply
of wood. A water bottle is essential:
drinking water is hard to find along
the stages. Binoculars are useful for
watching birds on the coast and the
whales that frequently appear off it.
Flippers and mask are also
recommended. Tsitsikamma is also
a marine reserve and a dive will offer
an interesting spectacle!
Access routes: the Tsitsikamma
National Park Visitor Centre at the
mouth of Storms River is reached
via a short detour from the coast
road that connects Cape Town to
Port Elizabeth, between Plettenberg
Bay and Humansdorp. The area is
easily accessible by bus.
Guides and porters: there are none.
Detours and peaks: the route is
compulsory. Before departure you
can follow one of the two nature

paths around the visitor centre.
The Tsitsikamma Trail, an interesting
trek in five stages, starts from
Nature's Valley and follows the
buttresses of the Outeniqua
Mountains, inland from Tsitsikamma.
Well-trained hikers can combine the
two treks.
In case of trouble: all the refuge huts
are easily reached from inland and
are equipped with emergency radios.
Maps: the best, available locally,
is the 1/50,000 scale map published
by the National Hiking Way Board.
Less detailed is the *Garden Route
map* published by Map Studio;
The Tsitsikamma Park is shown
on 1/100,000 scale.
Guidebooks: available locally is
the *The Otter Trail and the
Tsitsikamma Coastal National Park*
guidebook by Patrick Wagner.
The excellent *Best Hikes in South
Africa* by David Bristow (Struik,
1992) is full of useful information
but too bulky to be carried in
a rucksack.

*157 These cosy
bungalows in
Tsitsikamma
National Park are
located right on the*
*beach, one of the
loveliest spots of
South Africa.
Photograph by
Marc van Aardt*

FIRST DAY
from Storms River to Ngubu Hut
distance climbed: 200 metres
distance descended: 200 metres
time: 3 hours

SECOND DAY
from Ngubu Hut to Scott Hut
distance climbed: 350 metres
distance descended: 350 metres
time: 4 hours

158 top Situated not far from the eastern boundary of the Tsitsikamma National Park, the mouth of the Storms River is a splendid rocky gorge.
Photograph by Hein Von Horsten/A.B.P.L.

158 centre An attractive hanging bridge allows the trekker to cross Storms River.
Photograph by Mark van Ardt

Hikers directed towards the Otter Trail are welcomed with a short conference and a video at the Park Visitor Centre. From the chalets and the camp site, the path, marked with the characteristic "otter paws" in yellow, enters the thick vegetation of the coastal forest, descending to rocky coastline and passing the Guano Cave before climbing for a stretch and then descending to a lovely waterfall. It climbs again in the forest and returns to the coast and Ngubu Hut

Another not excessively tiring stage, offering an encounter with a splendid forest and lovely fern undergrowth. Start with a steep climb towards the Olienboomkop forest, crossing it to the magnificent natural scenic spot of Skilderkrans. A section overlooking the coast precedes the descent to the Kleinbos River, leaving a small path for the beach of Bloubaai to the left, and then climbs again to the highest altitude of the trek (about 150 metres). The last descent leads to the Geelhoutbos River and the attractive Scott Hut set on the edge of the forest.

158 right Seen from above, from the path leading to the Park Visitor Centre, the bridge over Storms River is even more spectacular.
Photograph by Stefano Ardito

THIRD DAY
from Scott Hut to Oakhurst Hut
distance climbed: 250 metres
distance descended: 250 metres
time: 4 hours

Another fairly short day with a prolonged and spectacular stretch on the impressive coastal cliffs. Start with a short section in the forest and return to the coast at Flipse Baai; you

158 bottom left The picture shows the rich vegetation characterizing the whole park and seen all along the trek.
Photograph by Mauro Burzio

FIFTH DAY
from André Hut to Nature's Valley
distance climbed: 250 metres
distance descended: 250 metres
time: 4 hours

The last day of the trek starts with the steep and exhausting climb to the plateau, upriver from the Martiense Bank cliffs, proceeding on an open and extremely scenic area. Descend to cross first a tributary and then the Helpmekaar River; you encircle a last rocky ravine and then descend along a sandy gorge. The splendid dunes of Nature's Valley mark the end of the loveliest possible adventure on the coasts of South Africa.

159 top The Otter Trail has numerous fords which lend adventure, as well as the opportunity of admiring a pristine nature, to the trek. In the photograph a party of trekkers is crossing the mouth of Bloukrans River, at the end of the fourth leg. Photograph by Anthony Bannister/ A.B.P.L.

159 centre On the first day the Otter Trail passes through some of the most spectacular rocky landscape of the Tsitsikamma coastline. Photograph by Athol Franz/ A.B.P.L.

159 bottom At sunset, the Tsitsikamma rocks and the waves of the Indian Ocean make a particularly spectacular, moving picture. Sometimes after a long wait, several species of whale can be sighted off the coast. Photograph by Eric Reisinger/A.B.P.L.

then climb over a rocky promontory to come to the beaches at the mouth of the Elandsbos River, one of the best places to spot the elusive Cape otter. A long stretch on the rocky coast with short detours inland follows. A tiring climb leads to the plateau from which you descend towards the Lottering River. A sometimes not elementary ford leads to Oakhurst Hut built a few dozen metres from the coast.
In summer a rather long detour inland is required to procure drinking water.

FOURTH DAY
from Oakhurst Hut to André Hut
distance climbed: 350 metres
distance descended: 350 metres
time: 5 hours 30 minutes

The fourth day is the longest and most tiring on the Otter Trail. As well as being almost 15 kilometres long, there are numerous ups and downs to be considered. You start with a long hike in a rather sparse forest and a series of tiring ascents and descents to pass the often dry streams. Two thirds of the way along the route you will come to the spectacular mouth of the Bloukrans River. At low tide this is forded without particular difficulties; at high tide and when the sea is rough a long wait may be necessary.
The path proceeds in the forest, descending to a stony beach and climbing again to the plateau, providing a sweeping view of Nature's Valley and Plettenberg Bay.
A last descent leads to the Klip River Valley and the refuge hut in the woods a few metres from the cliffs.

THE DRAKENSBERGS

The spectacular "Dragon's mountains"
on the border between Natal and Lesotho

Coasts and sunny savannah, forests of pine trees and protea in bloom. Lions and whales, rhinoceros and penguins. A country of splendour and contrasts, South Africa embraces a wide selection of mountains.

The highest are the Drakensbergs which mark the boundary between Natal and the independent state of Lesotho. They owe their name to the first Boer trekkers who named them Drakensberg, "the mountains of the dragons". The Zulu called them and still do so *Quathlamba*, the "barrier of spears". Here, even the most demanding and expert mountain-lover will feel at home. With its faces and solitary peaks, the highest chain in South Africa reaches 3,400 metres and offers its visitors a remarkable sequence of majestic rocky faces, deep chasms eroded by rivers, caves used for centuries as shelter by the hunting tribes of the area and decorated with interesting drawings by the artists of the distant past.

On the paths surprises are many. Climbing towards the plateau that hosts the Tugela springs, the great Zulu river, the sudden appearance of a bearded vulture is an outstanding welcome to the chain: many other vultures will be sighted later on. High up, on the meadows, you will encounter rheeboks, small graceful antelopes intent on grazing. Baboons are also common on the Drakensbergs. Disturbed by our steps on the path to the metal steps of Mont-aux-Sources, a tribe of these monkeys chooses a dihedron of at least fourth degree for its escape. From the lowlands of Natal and Qwazulu, the Drakensbergs seem to bar the horizon. Within sight of the bizarre rocks of this chain for seventy years and more there was a succession of the most cruel skirmishes and battles in the history of South Africa. In February 1838, a colony of Boer settlers from the Cape, at the end of their "Great Trek", were massacred by the Zulus of the king Dingaane at Weneen. Ten months later the settlers had their revenge on

the river Nkome, since then known as Blood River. In 1879 a Zulu army of 25,000 men made a surprise attack on the British army camp at Isandlwana, killing all the defenders and inflicting on Queen Victoria's armies one of the heaviest defeats ever suffered by the white settlers in Africa. Later, in the two Anglo-Boer wars the two white "tribes" of South Africa fought each other in the sunny hills of the Zulu land. The mountains, however, have always been a place of peace and tranquillity, as well as the boundary between two very different worlds. Spread over two hundred kilometres or more the chain is actually the edge of the Lesotho plateau - a world of rocks, mountain pastures and woods - overlooking the Natal plain, the distant beaches around Durban and on the Umfolozi, Hluhluwe and Mkuzi savannahs populated by rhinoceros, wildebeest, giraffes and zebras.

On the slopes of these mountains the clouds of the Indian Ocean turn into rain. Great cliffs of sandstone, singular pinnacles and canyons create an extraordinary landscape. On the plateau the helichrysum are reminiscent of Mounts Kilimanjaro and Kenya. In the valley shelters and caves conserve the antelopes, elephants and warriors drawn by the San, the mountain tribes driven to extinction by the arrival of the new black and white ethnic groups. Some of the Drakensberg peaks (among these Mont-aux-Sources from which the Tugela, Elands River and Khubedu are born) are actually on the edge of the rolling Lesotho plateau. Others (including the Sentinel Peak 3,165 metres, Cathedral Peak 3,004 metres, Champagne Castle 3,377 metres) are impressive, detached rock towers. There is no lack of pinnacles, such as the Devil's Tooth, the Sentinel and the Bell: formed from crumbling sandstone these peaks are of no particular appeal to mountaineers. There are numerous destinations for hikers. In the Royal Natal National Park (the northernmost area) are the Tugela gorges and the

160-161
On the boundary between the Natal savannah and the Lesotho plateau, the harsh mountain *range of the Drakensbergs (here seen from the air) offer an encounter with the wildest* *mountain environment in southern Africa.* Photograph by Herman Potgieter/ A.B.P.L.

walls of the Amphitheatre. The Mont-aux-Sources plateau can be reached from the nearby Qwa Qwa homeland. The Cathedral Peak Hotel and the Cathkin Park Hotel are the bases for the ascent to Cathedral Peak and Champagne Castle, the loveliest of the peaks accessible without difficulty. The loveliest San drawings are in caves and natural shelters in the Giant's Castle Nature Reserve, farther south. In the valleys a number of comfortable hotels have, since the beginning of the century, welcomed visitors from Johannesburg, Durban and the rest of the country. There are of course many options for trekkers. Among the best itineraries are the Two Passes Hike, within sight of Cathedral Peak and the less demanding Two Huts Trail at the foot of Giant's Castle. Both take between three and four days. Other possibilities exist in many parts of the chain, in particular between the Royal Natal National Park and Mont-aux-Sources. We describe two separate treks. The first is of great scenic interest and more civilized thanks to the existence of roads and buildings. The second - in an equally spectacular area - is particularly suited to backpacking and wilderness enthusiasts.

USEFUL INFORMATION

Duration: 5 days for the trek to Mont-aux-Sources, 4 days for the Cathedral Peak circuit.

Elevation: from 1,400 to 3,282 metres for the Roal Natal National Park, from 1,450 to 3281 metres for Cathedral Peak.

Period: hiking is possible all year round on the Drakensbergs, though the middle seasons are preferable. The summer is very hot with frequent thunderstorms: in this season the waterfalls are particularly spectacular. The austral winter, cold by South African standards, is easily tolerated by European hikers.

Red tape: no visa is required for South Africa.

The first trek is open to a limited number (100 people in all). You must register at the Visitor Centre at the entrance to the Park or with the Natal Parks Board P.O. Box 662 Pietermaritzburg, Tel. (0027) (331) 471981 where you can also book nights in tents or bungalows in the Royal Natal National Park.

Degree of difficulty: steep stretches and some passages with metal steps on the climb to the Mont-aux-Sources plateau and Cathedral Peak. Otherwise only steep path with no true difficulties.

Physical challenge: average-high because of the altitude, the size of the rucksack and the steep stretches. The humid summer heat complicates matters.

Equipment: the first trek does not require a tent, you can sleep in the bungalows of the Witsieshoek Resort and Tendele Camp; the second is in a wilder environment but can, nonetheless, be followed using the numerous caves along the way for the night and thus saving the weight of a tent. Normal mountain gear is required with a good protection against the rain. A rope is useful to secure inexpert trekkers on the steep metal stairs.

Access routes: the roads to the Drakensbergs branch off the Johannesburg-Durban motorway between Harrismith and the Mobi River. The Royal Natal National Park is reached via Bergville and the Oliviershoek Pass: leave your car at the car park near the Visitor Centre (1,400 metres). The Cathedral Peak

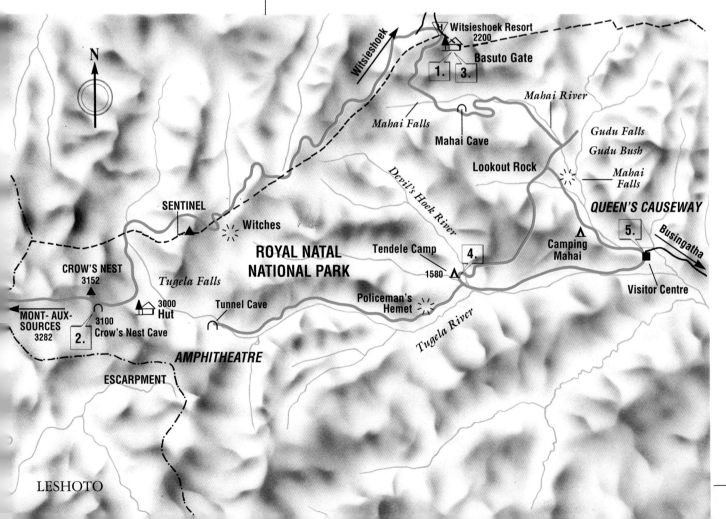

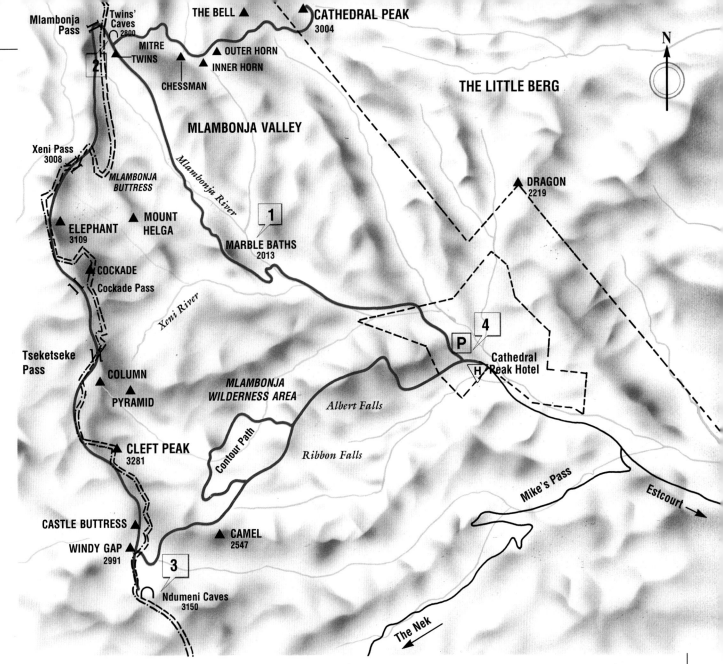

THE BELL ▲ ▲ CATHEDRAL PEAK
3004

Mlambonja Twins'
Pass Caves
2800

MITRE ▲ OUTER HORN
TWINS ▲ INNER HORN
CHESSMAN ▲

THE LITTLE BERG

MLAMBONJA VALLEY

Mlambonja River

N

Xeni Pass
3008

MLAMBONJA
BUTTRESS

DRAGON
2219

▲ MOUNT
HELGA

ELEPHANT
3109

COCKADE
Cockade Pass

Xeni River

1

MARBLE BATHS
2013

4

P

Tseketseke
Pass

COLUMN
PYRAMID

MLAMBONJA
WILDERNESS AREA

Albert Falls

Cathedral
Peak Hotel
H

CLEFT PEAK
3281

Contour Path

Ribbon Falls

CASTLE BUTTRESS

Mike's Pass

Estcourt →

WINDY GAP
2991

3

▲ CAMEL
2547

Ndumeni Caves
3150

The Nek

sector is reached from Winterton: leave the car in the public car parks before the Cathedral Peak Hotel (1,450 metres).

Guides and porters: there are no porters. Accompanied and guided hikes in the Drakensbergs are organized by various agencies and associations in Johannesburg, Pretoria, Durban and Pietermaritzburg.

Detours and peaks: the itineraries described include some of the most interesting peaks in the Drakensbergs, e.g. Mont-aux-Sources (3,282 metres), Cathedral Peak (3,004 metres) and Cleft Peak (3,281 metres). Many others can be included with short detours.

In case of trouble: contact the personnel of the protected areas. Help is generally fast to arrive, often with the use of helicopters.

Maps: the 1:50,000 map *North Drakensberg* published by the

Directorate of Forestry includes both itineraries. For the first there is also the 1:20,000 map *Royal Natal National Park - Mont-aux-Sources* available locally.

Guidebooks: locally you can find the book *Royal Natal National Park* and *Rugged Glen Nature Reserve* (Natal Parks Board). The excellent *Best Hikes in South Africa* by David Bristow (Struik, 1992) is brimming with useful information but too bulky to go in the rucksack.

For general details on the country we suggest *South Africa, Lesotho and Swaziland* by R. Everist and J. Murray (Lonely Planet, 1993).

For further reading: among the most interesting books are *Natal and the Zulu Country* by T.V. Bulpin (Books of Africa), *Barrier of Spears* by R.O. Pearse and *The Rock Art of South Africa* by A.R. Wilcox (Nelson).

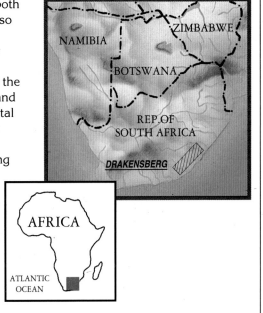

NAMIBIA

ZIMBABWE

BOTSWANA

REP. OF
SOUTH AFRICA

DRAKENSBERG

AFRICA

ATLANTIC
OCEAN

FROM ROYAL NATAL NATIONAL PARK
TO MONT-AUX-SOURCES

FIRST DAY
from the Visitor Centre
to Witsieshoek
distance climbed: 800 metres
time: 5 hours

From the Visitor Centre proceed
on foot along the asphalt road, pass
the Mahai camping site and continue
along the path leading to the
Queen's Causeway and the lovely
waterfalls of the Mahai river.
The path proceeds with a very steep
stretch to the left and near Lookout
Rock reaches another easier path.
Follow this crossing the river to
Gudu Bush (possible detour to the
waterfalls of the same name) and
continue to climb the valley passing
the Mahai Cave and the beautiful

Mahai Falls. A climb across to
the right will take you to the
Basuto Gate and Witsieshoek
(2,200 metres) where you can
spend the night.

SECOND DAY
from Witsieshoek
to Crow's Nest Cave
distance climbed: 550 - 850 metres
time: 4 - 6 hours 30 minutes

A long and absolutely stunning
day leading to the plateau above
the great Escarpment, clearly visible
from the Royal Natal Hotel and the
Visitor Centre. You should most
certainly try to find a lift to the
end of the road (2500 metres,
9 kilometres, 2 hours 30 minutes

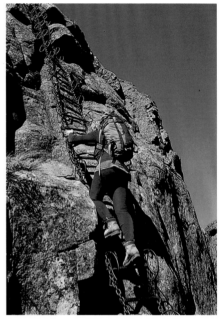

164 left
The singular
sentinel tower
(3,165 metres)
dominates the path
that climbs to the
Mont-aux-Sources
plateau.
Photograph by
Stefano Ardito

164 top right
The last stretch of
the path up towards
the Mont-aux-
Sources plateau

involves a climb on
a long, impressive
metal ladder.
Photograph by
Stefano Ardito

164 bottom right
The three leaps of
the Tugela Falls, the
highest and most
spectacular in South
Africa, seen from the
edge of the plateau.
Photograph by
Roger de la Harpe/
A.B.P.L.

FIFTH DAY

from Tendele Camp to Tugela Tunnel and from Tugela Tunnel to the Visitor Centre
distance climbed: 700 metres
distance descended: 880 metres
time: 6 hours

Splendid and wild, the chasm followed by the Tugela River - already admired from the edge of the Escarpment - adds the final touch to the trek. A steep descent leads to the main path then followed across the mountain, parallel to the river. A long crossing at the foot of the Policemen's Helmet Rocks will take you to the narrowest stretch of the gorges, where the Tugela must be crossed three times. Cross it using the natural tunnel (getting wet) or go round this to the right on metal steps.
A last climb leads to the mouth of Tunnel Cave, a splendid viewpoint over the Amphitheatre. Return as you came. At the end, after leaving the climb to Tendele Camp to the left, continue on the flat to the road and the point of departure.

on foot) and a construction used by the Park rangers. A broad path continues along a number of bends leaving, to the left, the spectacular Sentinel tower, skirts walls and will take you to a saddle. Once past the quite breathtaking metal steps, proceed on the plateau to a refuge hut (3,000 metres), now only used as a surveillance station and closed to the public. The alternative for the night is Crow's Nest Cave (3,100 metres reached by climbing for another 30 minutes). The edge of the Escarpment, a few minutes from the refuge hut, offers a sensational view at dawn or sunset. Here the spectacular Tugela Falls plunge down into the void towards the Amphitheatre.

THIRD DAY

from Crow's Nest Cave to Witsieshoek
distance climbed: 250 metres
distance descended: 1,150 metres
time: 6 hours 30 minutes

A long stage that starts with the climb to the nearby Crow's Nest (3,152 metres) and then proceeds along a broad, easy ridge to the Mont-aux-Sources peak (3,282 metres, 2 hours return). Back at the cave, take the crosswise route to the outward path and follow this to the road and Witsieshoek Resort. If you manage to hitch a lift you will save two hours. Trained hikers can return directly to the valley bottom.

FOURTH DAY

from Witsieshoek Resort to Tendele Camp
distance climbed: 100 metres
distance descended: 720 metres
time: 4 hours

The stage leading to the bottom of the valley can be covered without haste, getting to know the valley, stopping for a swim in one of the rivers and going to the Gudu Falls. Leave the path for the Queen's Causeway to the left and keep to the right at the forks and you will come to Tendele Camp (1,580 metres) where you can stay the night in a bungalow.

AROUND CATHEDRAL PEAK

166 top A group of Zulu huts not far from the road between Winterton and the Cathedral Peak Hotel. Cathedral Peak (3,004 metres) appears in the background. Photograph by David Keith Jones/ Images of Africa Photobank

166 centre The wide river shore with, in the background, the Champagne Castle massif (3,377 metres) in the central Drakensbergs. Photograph by David Keith Jones/Images of Africa Photobank

166 bottom A group of trekkers rests on a path in the Drakensbergs. In the background is the rounded Indanyana Peak. Photograph by David Keith Jones/Images of Africa Photobank

167 top left The light of dawn reddens Cathedral Peak (3,004 metres) seen here in a stunning aerial view. Photograph by Stefano Ardito

167 bottom left Foaming waters greet trekkers at the end of the descent near the Mike's Pass road. Photograph by Nigel Dennis/A.B.P.L.

167 top right A group of trekkers admires the peaks of the Eastern Buttress (3,047 metres) and Devil's Tooth from the start of the path that climbs from Witzieshoek Resort and Kwa Kwa to Mont-aux-Sources. Photograph by Roger de la Harpe/A.B.P.L.

167 bottom right Another aerial view showing the massive faces of the Elephant (3109 metres) and Cleft Peak (3281 metres), south of Cathedral Peak. Photograph by Stefano Ardito

168 Mawenzi (5149 metres), a spectacular rocky satellite of Kilimanjaro, is one of the most "alpine" peaks on the African continent. Photograph by Didier Givois

FIRST DAY
from the Cathedral Peak Hotel to Mlambonja Valley distance climbed: 650 metres time: 3 hours 30 minutes

Not long but with interesting views, the first stage of the trek allows you to start the climb to the rocky face and the Drakensberg peaks without too much effort.
Trained hikers will proceed to Twins Cave, thus having a full day to dedicate to the aerial and spectacular route to Cathedral Peak. Go from the car park to the hotel and proceed along the easy path beside the Mlambonja River; leave the deep Xeni River Valley to the left, climb to the left and then return to the river at Marble Baths (2,013 metres) where you can camp comfortably.

SECOND DAY
from Mlambonja Valley to Cathedral Peak and the Twins' Pass distance climbed: 800-1,000 metres distance descended: 100-300 metres time: 4-6 hours

A lovely and varied stage on which you can climb steep exposed stretches to Cathedral Peak or stop on the ridge preceding it.
After leaving the camp, start again to climb the gradually steeper valley. Cross the stream and go round a spur, then proceed at the foot of the Inner Horn, Chessman and Mitre rock towers to the saddle between the Twins and the main Drakensberg face. Just beyond this are the remarkable Twins' Caves (2,800 metres) where twenty or so people can spend the night. It is best to leave your camping gear and continue eastwards on the path that skirts the Mitre, Inner Horn and Outer Horn chain to the north and return to the ridge at the foot of The Bell, one of the most graceful peaks in the chain. A fairly aerial crossing takes the path to the southern slope of Cathedral Peak and then climbs to the top (3,004 metres).
The return journey is by the same route.

THIRD DAY

*from Twins' Pass
to Cleft Peak and Windy Gap
distance climbed: 700 - 950 metres
distance descended: 510 - 760 metres
time: 5 - 7 hours*

A long and particularly spectacular day on which you will skirt the edge of the Escarpment at length, climbing if you wish to the scenic Cleft peak. You start with a steep climb to the Mlambonja Pass (2,980 metres) where you come onto the plateau. From here on the route is not obligatory: keeping closer to the edge of the Escarpment you can admire the best views and reach the peaks. At the Xeni Pass (3,008 metres) go round or up to the Elephant

(3,109 metres), passing the Cockade and Tseketseke Passes, an excellent viewpoint over the rocky Column and Pyramid Peaks. A steeper ascent leads to the panoramic Cleft Peak (3,281 metres) from where you proceed down to Windy Gap (2,991 metres). You can camp here or go on up to the uncomfortable Ndumeni Caves (3,150 metres).

FOURTH DAY

*from Windy Gap to the
Cathedral Peak Hotel
distance descended: 1,590 metres
time: 4 hours*

This long descent, rather hard on the legs, can be alleviated by leaving a car in advance at the barrier at the end of Mike's Pass road. Start by keeping left at a fork, reaching the Camel ridge (2,547 metres), dominated by the Castle Buttress rocks, and proceed to (2,100 metres) the cart track of Contour Path. Follow this for a little to the left and then descend again along the path overlooking a deep ravine; this offers a lovely view of Ribbon Falls and Albert Falls before proceeding to the Cathedral Park Hotel and the car park.

Cover
Set on a ridge separating equatorial Africa from the savannah, Ruwenzori offers a rich botanic assortment: from lush rain forests to clearings dotted with towering heather and giant lobelia.
Photograph by Stefano Ardito

Back cover - top
The climb to Punta Margarita in Ruwenzori crosses the Stanley Plateau, dominated by the black rocks of the Moebius in a seemingly alpine landscape.
Photograph by Stefano Ardito

Back cover - bottom
The splendid dune of the eastern Grand Erg just a few hours march from the Tassili-n-Ajjer massif at the edge of the Algerian Sahara is a constantly changing natural work of art.
Photograph by Mario Verin

The publisher and author would like to thank the following for their valuable assistance: African Explorer, Air Algerie, Air Zaire, Arca, Caravan, Ethiopian Airlines, Kel 12, Kenya Wildlife Service, Kibo Hotel, Lufthansa, Moroccan Ministry for Tourism, Naro Moru River Lodge, Rhino Safaris, Royal Air Maroc, Sabena, Satour, South African Airways, Tanzania Tourist Corporation, Tourisport.

Special thanks also go to: Alberto Addis, Fabiana Cannizzaro, François Chalumeau, Cristiano Delisi, Samia Saleh Kebire, Lydia Martinuzzi, Franco Pecci, Alessandro and Franco Simonetti, Liz Swart.